John Grierson and the NFB

JOHN
GRIERSON
and the NFB

The John Grierson Project
McGill University

ECW PRESS

John Grierson and the NFB has been published with the assistance of a grant from The John Grierson Project, McGill University. Additional grants have been provided by the Ontario Arts Council and The Canada Council.

The cover photograph of John Grierson is courtesy of the NFB. The cover was designed by The Dragon's Eye Press. *John Grierson and the NFB* was typeset by Imprint Typesetting, and printed by Hignell.

Published by ECW PRESS, 307 Coxwell Avenue, Toronto Ontario.

Canadian Cataloguing in Publication Data

Main entry under title:
John Grierson and the NFB

Papers presented at a conference held at McGill University, Montreal, Quebec, Oct. 29-31, 1981.
ISBN 0-920802-80-X

1. Grierson, John 1898-1972 – Congresses.
2. Moving-picture producers and directors – Great Britain – Biography – Congresses. 3. Moving-pictures, Documentary – Canada – History – Congresses.
4. National Film Board of Canada – History – Congresses.

PN1998.A.3G7135 1984   791.43'0232'0924   C84-098481-2

CONTENTS

John Grierson

JOHN GRIERSON was born near Stirling, Scotland, in April, 1898 and died in Bath, England, in February, 1972. The vitality and vision of this small, dynamic man made him a giant in film history. His influence has been felt by generations of film-makers and his concepts have shaped the course of the documentary film, a term he coined.

Son of scholarly parents, Grierson was an outstanding student at Glasgow University. He began his career as a lecturer in English and Moral Philosophy at Durham University and ended it as visiting professor at McGill University in Montreal. In between came a life of achievement, fame, insight, warm friendships, bitter enmity, and much turbulence. His university education was interrupted by the First World War, where he served on a minesweeper in the North Sea. Returning to university, he received a Master of Arts in 1923, and proceeded to lecture at Durham. He won a Rockefeller Research Fellowship to Chicago University in 1924 and spent three years in the United States studying the psychology and effects of the mass media. While there he formed his concepts on film as an instrument of social change and developed the idea of wedding aesthetics, realism and idealism. He wrote later, "Art is not a mirror; it is a hammer." He wrote about film in the U.S. press and while reviewing *Moana*, a 1926 film by Robert Flaherty, he suggested it had "documentary value," for the first time using the term "documentary" in relation to the depiction of everyday reality on film. Grierson's later definition of documentary film as "the creative treatment of actuality" has been widely quoted ever since.

In 1927 Sir Stephen Tallents invited him to help convince the Empire Marketing Board in Great Britain that film was a viable form of information and promotion. He made *Drifters*, a 50-minute documentary about the livelihood of the North Sea fishermen. His success enabled him to gather together a small group of enthusiastic young men eager to learn film-making. When the EMB Film Unit dissolved in 1933, the group joined the General Post Office Film Unit, where such documentary classics as *Song of Ceylon* and *Night Mail* were made. Initially requested to advise on the state of film production in Canada and Australia, Grierson was subsequently employed by Prime Minister Mackenzie King, just prior to the outbreak of the Second World War, to coordinate Canadian film activities. The National Film Board was founded, to "tell Canadians about their country and to inform the world about Canada." The war occasioned the additional development of the Wartime Information Board under Grierson's direction, and before long the NFB was producing between 200-300 films a year, including the acclaimed "Canada Carries On" and "World in Action" series as well as the academy-award-winning *Churchill's Island* and *The War for Men's Minds*.

At the end of the war, Grierson attempted to organize a commercial film group in New York but was caught up in the cold war hysteria of the time. Because an NFB secretary had been named in a Russian document brought to light by the Gouzenko trials, J. Edgar Hoover turned the full force of the FBI investigation squad against Grierson and wrote to President Harry S. Truman urging his expulsion. Grierson's visa was cancelled as U.S. newspapers trumpeted "Spy Suspect Expelled." (A Canadian politician had already complained that Grierson was an "out-and-out CCF follower"!) Grierson left Canada for England.

At this low point, Julian Huxley, the Director-General of UNESCO in Paris, invited him to become the first Director of Mass Communications and public information for this new UN agency, but Grierson was never at ease in the role and the early fifties in Britain saw another frustrated attempt to develop government-sponsored commercial film-making, accompanied by periods of ill health. However, by 1955 Grierson was vigorously employed again with Films of Scotland, promoting the country he loved so much. Particularly successful was *Seawards the Great Ships* which received premier awards, and an Oscar. He participated extensively in international film festivals and during a trip across Canada he reviewed the National Film Board, strongly urging closer film and television ties between the NFB and the CBC. In 1957, the Scottish-Canadian newspaper magnate, Lord Thompson of Fleet, asked him to present a documentary television program, "This Wonderful World," for Scottish Television. Highly successful, the series ran ten years. When it concluded, Grierson became visiting professor at McGill. Three years later, during university Christmas break in 1971, he holidayed at his country home near Bath. There he fell mortally ill.

This man who had done so much for Canada and for film-making worldwide had received many honours, including the Golden Thistle at the Edinburgh Festival, an honourary LLD from Glasgow University and the CBE, but he had never received an honour from Canada. As Grierson lay dying, the principal of McGill was trying to reach him by phone to say Grierson had been chosen to receive an honourary doctorate. The principal was too late.

Grierson's greatest honour has been the respect and affection of students, film-makers, and colleagues throughout the world. His influence on film-making has been enormous; one of his monuments is the National Film Board of Canada.

> "The greatest export of the Film Board has been the Film Act itself. It's been translated into many languages, it's become the model of serious intention by the cinema in the service of government, all over the world. The success of the Film Board has been in its helping [the Department of] External Affairs to present the Canadian capabilities. The Film Board has been important in saying to countries of very different kinds, all over the world, that *the film is an instrument of great importance in establishing the patterns of the national imagination.*"
>
> —John Grierson, interviewed by James Beveridge for the NFB film *John Grierson* (1972)

PETER OHLIN

Introduction

SOME FORTY-ODD YEARS after the National Film Board of Canada
came into being, a federal commission reviewing cultural policy
has, in all seriousness, suggested virtually dismantling the organization. There is a kind of odd poetic justice about this: all things
must come to an end — even, perhaps, government institutions
(though they very rarely recognize this themselves, which is why
the suggestion is bound to appear so rude). The National Film
Board was created by John Grierson at a specific time and place,
and part of its success was surely due to the man (and all those who
served him), the time, and the place. The man is gone now, and the
time and the place are no longer the same. Granted its excellence in
the making of documentaries, can an institution like the Film
Board renew itself to deal with the changing cultural climate? How
does an institution renew itself? How does anyone define the
changing rôle of central social institutions? Is the rôle itself as
necessary as it was forty years ago?

These questions, perhaps unnecessarily pointed here, are obviously for others to answer. But the issue itself is quite clearly the
kind that John Grierson would have enjoyed and treated with some
passion. And the urgency with which these questions are asked
now testifies to the continuing importance of those issues that
appear with such force and energy throughout Grierson's work.
The importance of that work rests not just on the concrete
achievements duly noted in any history of the cinema (the documentary movement, the creation of the NFB, and so on), but in the
demonstration of the available possibility of a concrete cultural
action. That possibility — that is, the conviction that a nation can
or should be able to take control of its own culture, in the fullest
sense of that word — has come to seem increasingly important in
the Canadian cultural context in the last few years.

I

Let me suggest some examples:

First, in the light of current surveys of Canadian culture, it may not be inappropriate to suggest that the documentary is the essential Canadian form. It may, in fact, lead a productive life in other lands (and media) as well, but for many people the form itself is the only one that can be seen as an appropriate response to Canadian needs and resources. Critics as different as Bruce Elder and Northrop Frye (in his suggestion that the overwhelming question for a Canadian writer is not "Who am I?" as in the United States, but rather "Where is Here?") have agreed on the Canadian concern with documentation, map-making, landscape painting (the Group of Seven), and so on. In Canada, then, life is a kind of marginal existence on the outskirts of the major cultural movements, and resources must be assessed accordingly. It may be that it is not, in fact, a Canadian task to compete with American media, with Hollywood, but to struggle with documentation of regionalisms and similar perceptions. When Grierson created the NFB, one can suggest, he did not just create an institution for the making of a certain kind of film: he created an institutional embodiment of a number of different drives, needs, and purposes that, as James Beveridge so eloquently has pointed out, already existed in the country.

In fact, of course, the realization of this kind of "marginal" rôle inevitably brings with it a recognition of alternate forms of communication within the community itself: regionalisms, feedback and access programs of various kinds, neo-federalisms, and so on. In the face of various international monolithic pressures, such programs assume increasing significance.

Another, perhaps equally important, issue is connected with the complex of problems surrounding information, education, and the press. Grierson's practical insight, that there were more seats outside the movie theaters than in them, remains quite crucial. It is certainly true today that there are more learning opportunities outside the classroom than in it. And certainly the young today receive the major part of their education through the media, not through the schools. In such a situation it is criminal not to try to exercise some control over these "information" channels, and Grierson's constant preoccupation with information and propaganda as crucial instruments of public education remains as important today as it was during World War Two.

The scholars and film-makers who came to McGill in October 1981 to open the Grierson Project with a conference on John Grierson and his work addressed these and other important issues. What stood out particularly was that, while it was openly admitted that everyone who ever met Grierson was indelibly touched by the extraordinary dynamic and energizing presence of the man, it was infinitely more important to speak of the issues rather than of the man. What anecdotal information there was appeared in support of the arguments themselves. In other words, the conference participants heeded well Forsyth Hardy's opening remarks that to be true to Grierson we must at all costs avoid complacency.

The conference papers ranged freely among the issues concerned with Grierson. One group of papers dealt primarily with analyses of some of Grierson's work placed within the history of the documentary movement: Forsyth Hardy discussed Grierson's concern with democracy in action as expressed in an unpublished manuscript; Basil Wright discussed, from personal experience, some of the relationships between the British and Canadian documentary film-makers during World War Two, as did Jack Ellis; Jim Beveridge presented a masterly analysis of the Canadian network of people and resources that confronted Grierson when he arrived in Canada; and Eleanor Beattie documented with great care Grierson's attempt to move from documentary to fiction with an example from Cinema 3.

Another group of papers discussed more specific issues within film studies, like the theory of representation, the craft of film-making, and its social and moral implications; Ian Lockerbie presented some issues and statements in relation to Grierson and realism; Colin Low placed Grierson's teaching in the context of a larger sense of community; and Tom Daly discussed issues of craft not as a matter of technique, but as a matter of human growth.

Still another group of papers, finally, discussed Grierson's work as a kind of moral imperative within the contemporary situation: Rodrigue Chiasson's treatment of ethical elements in Grierson tapes for the CRTC belongs here; and Edgar and Daphne Anstey and Margaret Ann Elton were concerned with the work that remains to be done, within the framework of Grierson's practice, in fields like the Third World, education, and information.

As a whole, then, the conference demonstrated with considerable clarity that, while the documentary may have undergone many transformations since then, the Griersonian theory and practice of documentary has an ongoing significance not just in the specific Canadian context, but in the context of contemporary international media and the issues they provoke.

EDGAR AND DAPHNE ANSTEY

Grierson as a Stimulator of Third-World Communications

OUR LAST CONVERSATION with John Grierson took place in 1971 at the presentation dinner for the Canadian Film Awards at the Royal York Hotel in Toronto. Edgar was a member of the international jury and we sat at Grierson's table. The National Film Board won almost all of the awards and Edgar made a speech giving the credit for this to Grierson's pioneering influence. Meanwhile John — impatient as always with such backward-looking sentimentalities — talked to me about his recent visit with Len Chapman and Ken McCready to India.

Because of my activity in several international non-governmental organizations, I was a sitting target. He told me that such bodies too often seem to be blind and deaf to the role of communications technology, especially in rural areas where they could play a vital role. One of the organizations with which I work, the Associated Country Women of the World, has nine million members in some three hundred societies from over sixty countries, including Asia, Africa, and South America. Our affiliated societies in the developing world run projects on primary health care, clean water supply and sanitation, nutrition, literacy and basic education. We have for many years used flannel-graphs and posters and, more recently, battery-powered slide projectors to illustrate this work, but more sophisticated techniques are not easy to come by. Grierson's suggestions were — as always — forceful and stimulating. He wanted more government aid to promote involvement in an overall communications system within each country; and today I wonder if anything has come of his great plan whereby villages might bring alive their own problems with their own moving images. Or is it still only a dream?

I am pleased, however, that another organization with which I am concerned, the Commonwealth Human Ecology Council (CHEC) does hope to make a film about the need to subsidize "self-help" in the villages of Bangladesh rather than finance the centralized bureaucracy of aid; and there seems to be a fair chance that the National Film Board will be involved. It may be the first in a series envisaged by UNESCO titled "Man and His Habitat."

There is a multiple Grierson connection here. Edgar went out to Bangladesh for the World Bank a few years ago to advise on the reorganisation of social film-making there. CHEC has been involved in the promotion of this particular film, which is about the importance of local grass-roots initiative in development. Alex Shaw, another Grierson man, has helped a great deal through the World Bank.

Edgar and I are seriously worried about what happened, or rather what didn't happen, at Cancun last week in Mexico. Perhaps some of the inspiration and passion may have gone out of documentary work for the Third World in the past ten years. It would be wonderful if this seminar would prove us wrong.

Let us now look briefly at the record. Grierson's ambition to make a new language available to society always extended to the Third World. The fact that he started in the Empire Marketing Board gave him immediate contact with half the globe. Basil Wright's *Song of Ceylon* could quite appropriately have been shown in Mexico this week, and might have served to remind Ronald Reagan that the "Voices of Commerce" do not express the quality of an ancient but materially impoverished people as eloquently as does the beauty of their culture.

Empire Marketing Board became General Post Office later, but the tradition of creatively interpreting the exotically primitive was never lost. Documentary's missionaries emptied their tankards in the Highlander and set forth for Labrador, Africa, and the Caribbean. In the late thirties, Grierson's connection with the Imperial Relations Trust tended to concentrate his attention on Canada, Australia, and New Zealand. Edgar remembers how the threat of war in 1939 deprived him of a Grierson-inspired opportunity to go to Kabul to advise the Afghanistan government on starting a documentary unit. Grierson never allowed a meeting with a foreign leader to pass without recommending that he 'bring himself alive' through film!

The war advanced the cause in unexpected ways. At its end, Ralph Elton was in Malaya with people from the Crown and the Army Film Units. A home-going United States official film enter-

6

prise was about to dispose of its photographic and laboratory equipment. Ralph persuaded the British High Commissioner to buy it, then he set up the Malayan Film Unit, which is still functioning for the independent government. The Colonial Film Unit, another Grierson and Crown-related enterprise, began to spawn units overseas, especially in Africa. It was manned by Crown staff members like Stewart MacAllister.

When Grierson wrote the pre-war report recommending the establishment of the Shell Unit, his own mind was clear that the technological and scientific films would provide a new educational *lingua franca* employable internationally. In the immediate post-war years, Shell and other oil companies established film units in Iran, Iraq, Venezuela, and Singapore. Most were staffed by Grierson-trained personnel. In Venezuela, Shell used film as a principal means of promoting an officially adopted policy of using oil revenue to diversify industry and provide modern social services. It was not so much Grierson's teaching that produced this unexpected enlightenment as the fact that he trained his filmmakers to bring to the level of full consciousness what might be called the hidden logic of history.

When he returned from North America to England after the war, Stuart Legg was ready to use the skills he had perfected during his work on the NFB's "World in Action" series, which examines aspects of the social forces at work, in peacetime. Through Arthur Elton, Shell provided the opportunity again by sponsoring several remarkable films on the work of United Nations agencies such as Food and Agriculture, and World Health.

These intelligent, dramatically written and edited films fulfilled an early ambition of Grierson "to make peace as exciting as war." Produced in the fifties and sixties, such documentaries as *Food or Famine* probably represented the best contribution the Grierson school has yet made to an articulation of Third-World problems. They were made with imagination and are never dull.

There are many distinguished Third-World documentaries that Grierson's connection made inspirational. There is Basil Wright's and Paul Rotha's *World Without End* made for UNESCO in the early fifties. In 1949, Hollywood awarded *Daybreak in Udi* an Oscar for documentary features. John Taylor produced it, and Terry Bishop directed it just before Crown was closed down.

Members of the Grierson group have, in general, continued to recognize the fact that civilization as we have sought it will not

7

survive unless the population-growth problems can be reconciled with the finite character of planetary resources. Nuclear war is liable to be the only fruit of national and international competition in material consumption. Documentary has contributed to the staff of several United Nations agencies. Following in Grierson's footsteps at UNESCO was Alex Shaw, a man who was notably successful. His work, first at UNESCO and then at the World Bank, has resulted in several Third-World countries adopting communication policies designed to point the way to survival. Mary Losey, for many years a close collaborator of Grierson, worked on films for the World Health Organization through a particularly fruitful period that brought in documentary colleagues from many countries to work and direct.

At the London International Film School, a group of Grierson's early colleagues are associated with film and television teaching. Ralph Bond is in charge of documentary. This may prove to be a valuable training ground for Third-World film-making, since this school had early links with the Colonial Film Unit, and has the highest proportion of students from Third-World countries of all Britain's film schools.

So the seeds scattered by John Grierson throughout the developing world have provided growth and occasional flowering. We need only think of HABITAT, the United Nations World Conference on Human Settlements held in Vancouver in 1976. More than two hundred and twenty Conference films and slides from participating governments and non-governmental organizations were shown. The NFB was closely involved, as they are today, especially in the Third World.

In spite of present-day activity in impoverished continents, Edgar and I feel that the Grierson contribution of 'creative interpretation' must be increased quickly if our audiences are to be moved as well as informed. Hence this paper, which is intended solely to provoke discussion — discussion that we hope may prove any pessimism to be unjustified.

LOUIS APPLEBAUM

The NFB in the 1940s

Lou Applebaum: AS MANY OF YOU have already said, the opportunity to be part of this environment is the experience of a lifetime, and I'm delighted to be here. I'm going to take my cue from Margaret Ann and muse a little bit about the early forties because I go back that far with the National Film Board.

Margaret Ann Elton: Tell us about the viola, Lou.

Applebaum: The viola story is a plot. I used to love writing for the violas, and did often. I don't know where that viola image came from, especially its femininity. We all look on our musical instruments in different ways and I certainly don't look on the viola as a feminine image.

This morning Professor Lockerbie raised a few interesting problems for me with the question of Grierson and realism. Grierson and music, though that may not have been his bag, creates a number of intellectual tensions for me because, in fact, they contradict each other in so many ways. In the very beginning, music was a critical element in the evolution of the Film Board. I found a little black book — a treasure, with a list of all the films and dates.

The National Film Board is vital to me because it created me. I came to the Film Board out of school, enamoured with film, and Grierson took me and shaped me entirely into what I am. I attribute my whole life to John Grierson. I started living in 1941. The Grierson faith in youth that you've heard about, Grierson's ability to take a bunch of untried, anxious, desperate, passionate youths, and to convert them into something else, is what really mattered. That's what happened to me. He made me, not only into a quasi-film-maker, as he made Tom Daly and Jim Beveridge and Bob Anderson into film-makers — he turned us into film-makers, and he turned us into public servants. The idea of contributing to society was something that he instilled in all of us.

So, I went after my first job, typically worried about Grierson, who was gruff and difficult. He put me in a difficult position immediately. He was a sort of a professional maverick, and he measured you by your ability to overcome difficult circumstances. I was about twenty-one years of age. Grierson said to me, "How much do you earn?" At that time, I was doing social work and earning about ten dollars a week. I gave some piano lessons, and earned another ten dollars a week, so I said, "eighty dollars." He said, "I'll give you forty." I said, "I'll take it." That was my first lie, and I'm glad I lied.

So I started to work for the National Film Board officially. I first came to the Film Board because, when I was studying in New York, I visited the World's Fair, where I saw two remarkable films. One had a score by Aaron Copeland and the other had a score by Virgil Thompson. I saw them maybe a hundred and six times because a friend of mine had a pass. He told me that Godfrey Rideout had just done a film for the National Film Board, and that's how I learned about it. Some people were making films just like the ones I saw in New York. I discovered my old friend, Sidney Newman, was working for the Film Board, and somehow my name was given to Graham McInnes, and he gave me my first film job.

It was called *Call For Volunteers*. When I took my first plane trip from Toronto to Ottawa, I went to John Street by taxi. There was that incredible saw-mill — I'll never forget it — it's now a beautiful green sward opposite the French embassy, but we mustn't ever forget that hive of creative energy. The elegant screening room was a little barn, which served as a recording studio, music-recording room, and screening room. It was the only room of any size, and it was shared by National Health and Welfare with the mice and the guinea pigs and the dead rats we used to find in the cutting room. A fantastic place! When I arrived in the screening room, it was dark. Graham McInnes was running rushes for *Call For Volunteers*. I sneaked in and sat down. Graham stood up and started looking at the film through his legs because, in the National Film Board in those days, you were just as likely to splice the material upside-down as not.

I did that score, and a second one. In July of 1942, I worked with Norman McLaren on one of his very early films, and I haven't seen this film for thirty-five years, I'm sure. We have the film here; it's about five minutes long, and I'm dying to see it again. It was recorded in Toronto. Now, here's *Dollar Dance*, by Norman McLaren.

Peter Harcourt asked about McLaren, and whether Grierson created the animation department as a sort of counter-force to realism and documentary. We have to appreciate the fact that we're talking about 1940, and about wartime. All McLaren's films were of that genre, and they were doing a specific job. There was no room for improvisation and the techniques were of a creative impulse. What was being animated was a clear, realistic, wartime message, a propaganda message, and McLaren, animation, and everybody were devoted to that one cause.

In those days, the man running the music department in the National Film Board was Ralph Apsey, an American. He left a year or two later to go back to Hollywood. He was a prominent music editor on the Hollywood scene, and was brought in, as many foreigners were, to help set up the operation, and to provide expertise, because there was precious little around. Maurice Blackburn was there. He was the first composer at the National Film Board. Lucio Agostini was working in Associated Screen News in Montreal, where we did our first recordings. Later we did recordings in Toronto, New York, and elsewhere, but, in those days, it was always the Associated Screen News. Lucio was involved with many of Stuart Legg's actions in "Canada Carries On."

So we learned about film-making. We did everything, you know. I spent as much time in the cutting room as I did up in the music room. Sometimes we wrote our music at home. We were all young and ambitious, and naturally we thought we could transform the world. I became personally involved with all the people who were at the National Film Board, and the people who became involved grew exponentially with each passing month. I did films for Stuart Legg and Guy Glover and Sidney Newman, and for Regan because, like the nagative cutters, the composers were involved with everybody and everything.

One of the people who Grierson invited, in addition to Flaherty, Basil Wright, Stuart, and Stanley Hawes, was a Dutchman named Joris Ivens, a great film-maker who made a film about the Canadian Merchant Marines called *Action Stations*, in November of 1942. By this time, I had a dozen or so feature films under my belt, and this was the big 1940's epic, the hit film of 1942.

As a composer, you play your sketches for the producer to make sure you're on the same wave-length, and I remember we had a lousy piano at the Film Board. The French Embassy, an elegant building, was built across the road on the guarantee that this blight of a saw-mill would be removed forthwith but, like all of the temporary buildings in Ottawa, it stayed on for many years. The French Embassy absolutely hated the National Film Board's location because it was an affront to its sensibilities. With great trepidation, we called up and asked, "Could we come across and use your piano for a while?" Somehow they agreed, so it was there, in the French Embassy, that we worked out the music for *Action Stations*.

Professor Lockerbie was talking about realism, about the need for, and the ability of, the camera in documentary to reveal truth. I believe that there was the same degree of need for self-effacement by the film-maker from the subject he was involved with. I recall a conversation with Joris Ivens, who had come to Canada with a rather important reputation for making a film about coal-mining. It was apparently a very significant film. He told me something important, something that has always stayed with me: "My problem in making that film was to prove that life was terrible and ugly and difficult and poor." That was the essence of his message — to show how terrible life is among the coal-miners, but as soon as he put a light on, and put the camera with a frame around it, the whole scene looked beautiful. Lighting makes beautiful pictures, so he had to spend lots of effort trying to turn what is essentially a beautiful picture about an allegedly ugly subject into an ugly picture. He said he couldn't do it. So, the idea of self-effacement of the film-maker is a delusion. In fact, you are always working with images, whether they're drawn one way or another. The essence of artistic messages, whether you try to remove yourself or not, remains. You may remove yourself intellectually, but you can't remove yourself artistically.

The question of montage and camera is another subject with which I have great difficulty. Ivens was saying that, as soon as I put the frame and certain kinds of chiaroscuro into my picture, I'm creating a poetic image, and enhancing it. I'm creating a new kind of reality from my point of view, and that's where I have the problem of music and reality. You're using the most unreal of idioms to enhance whatever message you're trying to give. Now I'm going to run the opening sequences of *Action Stations*.

+ IVENS + STORCK; «Misère dans le BORINAGE »

When we were doing the mix for this, it went on into the middle of the night. Tommy Tweed was the narrator, and when we finally finished the mix, we decided to have some fun. We went back to the sound-effects room and grabbed everything we could think of. It's a forty-minute film; the destroyer corners a submarine, and it's very tense. They go down into the submarine and we have ticking time-bombs that we think are going to blow up. The commander of the submarine and the commander of the corvette get into a fight — it was exciting stuff in those days. So we did a mix and, instead of realistic sound effects, we had everything from chickens to Tommy Tweed. We simply ran the film and threw in sound effects as we saw fit. We used records from film, improvised on Tommy's new narration. At the point where the commander of the corvette and the commander of the submarine get into a fight, the corvette commander hits the Nazi and Tommy Tweed says, because Grierson was sitting there, "Take that, you dirty Presbyterian bastard."

Grierson came around about three o'clock in the morning to help us with the recording and the narration. Joris Ivens took it to Hollywood and had it screened. There was a Hollywood producer, Lester Cowan, whose wife was a composer, a famous song-writer. She wrote "Willow, Weep For Me," and "Who's Afraid of the Big Bad Wolf?" Aaron Copeland, their friend, was at the screening. Since this was a film about the Canadian Merchant Marine, and Cowan was about to produce a film about the Swedish Merchant Marine — to star, believe it or not, Greta Garbo — they were at this screening. Cowan asked Copeland, "Is the music okay?" and Copeland must have said yes because I got a telegram saying would I come down to Hollywood and write the music for a Greta Garbo film about the Swedish Merchant Marine? So I was an expert about music and the Merchant Marine, you see. Actually I never made that film, but I have worked for Lester Cowan, and we're still close friends.

The litany of film titles goes on, you know, page after page. There was a reference to a Japanese film that Stewart Legg made just before Pearl Harbor. Shortly after Pearl Harbor, in 1944, he made a film, *Fortress Japan*. It illustrates something about the National Film Board, and Grierson, and music in context. Music can do a number of things in film. One of them is to establish geographical locale. If you want to talk about Greece, for instance, you play Greek music. This film obviously called for Japanese something-or-other. So I did some research into Japanese music. I became an expert on folk music of all kinds. You name the country and I've written some folk tunes because of the National Film Board.

So I wrote the music for a flute that was to be played out of tune, and for percussion played on various noisemakers, and for a piano, except that the piano wasn't to be played in the traditional way. This film music was recorded in the same studio at John Street, and I'll never forget the look on the face of a very dignified musician who came to his first National Film Board recording. He was the pianist at the Chateau Laurier trio. He came in grey-striped trousers and a formal vest. He walked into this barn, this hell-hole of a room, where I was setting up the percussion instruments. The flutist was Dirk Kepast, who has since become a producer at CBC. He was a young kid in those days, and a good flute player. He had been instructed how to play the flute out of tune. This poor pianist, in his very formal attire, walked into the room and looked at a piano that had been stripped because he was supposed to play it with a screwdriver, and do twangs and bangs and zips.

I'll never forget the look on his face. I handed him a screwdriver and said, "That's your piano." He was totally lost. What that film demonstrated in 1944 was that the idiom became an integral part of our musical thinking. We could record things separately. We could run things backwards. It became physical. Music was recorded on optical striation, and remember we're talking pre-magnetic. You youngsters don't know this pre-magnetic world and that, being physical, you could do all kinds of crazy things with it. You could cut it up very accurately. I remember some terrible splicings. We learned to do things with synthetic music in later years, but in those days, it was very ingenious, a novel approach. It was done because we realized that what film represented as a medium changed the way we thought about music. That was a very symphonic type of score you just heard, but many scores that we worked on could not have been called concert music. This was one of the early ways we tried to explore the medium.

I came across an article I wrote on documentary music for something in 1943 or 1944, which said that the most important thing in the film composer's work is probably the influence that the medium itself has on his musical thinking. At the Board, the composer was encouraged to think as a film-maker as well as a musician. The cutting-room paraphernalia was as familiar to him as his key signatures. Consideration of the microphone and splicing machine were as important as his concern with smooth key modulation. We used the microphone in *Fortress Japan* by waving it around in front of the flute player, in order to get a certain crazy, unnatural sound. He quickly realized that he was not writing music for concert performances, and therefore adjusted his conception of musical form accordingly. He learned the value of dramatic statement and effective orchestration.

ELEANOR BEATTIE

From Documentary to Fiction: A Study of John Grierson's Work in Group 3

GROUP 3, an investment-scheme project of the National Film Finance Corporation, set up in 1951, was designed to stabilize the British film industry. I will put aside the detailed history of how the British cinema attempted to protect itself. Ironically, its numerous reports, quotas, and protective laws often backfired.

Over the years, the struggle had been to make feature films that could be sold abroad but, failing that source of return, to protect a distinctive home production while giving work and training to youthful actors, directors, and technicians. Neither quota quickies nor Anglo-American co-productions were the answer. The formation of Group 3 was one significant attempt to fulfill these obligations. Using monies collected through the Eady Plan or the Entertainment Tax, Group 3 was part of a more extensive program to support feature film production companies. Three new film production groups were planned to work in conjunction with established studios: Group A was connected to the Rank organization; groups B and C with ABCP. By 1953, only Group C, now renamed Group 3, remained. Because of the low state of the industry at the time, unemployment, lack of opportunity for young talent, and the scheme's architects, Group 3's mandate was more significant than simply producing feature films for the seminal figures in (to use Tallents' phrase) "the projection of Britain." These included John Reith, formerly of the BBC and, in 1951, chairman of the National Film Finance Corporation; Michael Balcon, head of Ealing Studio, employer of many from Grierson's documentary school, producer of wartime fiction and, in 1951, NNFC nominee and chairman of Group 3; and of course, John Grierson, in 1951 appointed Group 3's Joint Head of Production. Charles Barr, in his study of Ealing, calls them "a trio of powerful figures in the creation, and the colouring of distinctively British media."

In spite of Group 3 being a feature film production company, Grierson's relationship to the documentary had everything to do with his appointment. Grierson's forceful personality, his production of articles and discussions on the power of documentary, his linking documentary to public interest, and his cajoling to keep the commercial boys at bay nurtured his film-makers in the documentary units. Answering the Cambridge Questionnaire, he claimed that the documentary movement was "a considered effort to mobilize an economic place for the serious film-maker within the politico-economic framework." He pointed out the steps involved: "a theoretical analysis of the possibility; a promotion of the idea; an involvement with the politico-economic power, and a certain participation in its management; a production and distribution process and organization of the machinery...."[1]

When Grierson arrived back in England after his stint with UNESCO, the Central Office of Information appointed him "controller of the C.O.I.'s film operations to co-ordinate the work of the Films Division and the Crown Film Unit, and to take overall charge of the planning, production and distribution of government films."[2] What happened to Crown was what Grierson had struggled against at GPO — an infiltration by the bureaucrats into the creative control of film-making, and the increasingly strident demands by the industry that "if government departments wished to have films made for their own purposes, they should contract with the trade in open competition."[3] As well, in the demands of the war, Crown had moved away from the documentary into feature film-making, albeit using documentary methods. Many film-makers who were formerly with Crown moved over to Rank or Korda's London Films, and especially to Balcon's Ealing.

But Grierson still hoped that documentary could be revived in Britain in spite of post-war defections:

My hopes in this matter are liable to be boundless: not for my own part in it but, if I may say so simply, because of the film stuff it can create and the influence it can have on our time. Not least among these hopes is the hope of finding and developing new talents....[4]

It was not to be. Grierson, however, was still a power to be reckoned with. His proven ability to operate in a compromising political position, to search out and train talent, to produce films cheaply, made him an unquestionable candidate for the executive position with Group 3.

He was to join forces with Michael Balcon of Ealing, the employer of so much of Grierson's talent and, therefore, an inheritor of the documentary tradition. Balcon, like Grierson, ran a tight ship, a kind of on-the-job film school. According to Harry Watt, who had joined Ealing from Crown,

> The move over to Ealing was quite painless. It was a small, compact, self-contained unit run on paternalistic, communal lines by Michael Balcon. Under him there were half a dozen directors and associated producers, who formed interchangeable teams to make specific pictures, and who, once they got the go-ahead, worked pretty much on their own.[5]

Alberto Cavalcanti, who led the move, echoes this claim:

> Mick invited me to Ealing to carry on making documentaries. I was as happy at Ealing as I had been at GPO. It was a good atmosphere in part because of the boys I took in such as Watt and Hamer.... The co-operation at Ealing was very similar to that at the GPO.[6]

These quotes tell us why, as Barr says, "the 'documentary' and 'fiction' sides of Ealing interpenetrated so rapidly. Cavalcanti and Harry Watt joined fiction directors to combine propaganda punch and dramatic adaptation of a true story."[7] Balcon saw the documentary influence in Ealing films as an important aspect of planting his work firmly in English soil. Discussing dramas directed by Pen Tennyson, he said,

> The three films with Tennyson had dealt with problems in two cases social and one wartime, and so in a sense rendered a public service. They were documentary in their approach, but here I must define the term and establish that "documentary" is not a label to be lightly attached to films of a specific, factual type: it is an attitude of mind toward filmmaking. I had known at the back of my mind since *Man of Aran* that this was and should be the direction my own work should take.[8]

The definition of "documentary" is vague and romantic perhaps, but never mind; Balcon did hire Cavalcanti and Watt and, from wartime Ealing, films like *Nine Men*, *Next of Kin*, and *Went the Day Well* were made.

But after the war, Ealing moved from dramatized documentaries into ghost stories and comedies:

> *Hue and Cry* is a good example of what became the Ealing formula of placing eccentric or fantastic happenings in a realistically treated setting. The film's background of London streets and bomb sites is authentic.[9]

Roy Armes presses the point that the documentary element of Ealing's post-war films is "no more than a background element, the villains are unrelated to any contemporary social situation and the comedy arises from oddity rather than social contradiction."[10]

In spite of Ealing's move away from documentary-based drama, Balcon's work in Group 3 revived that strain. This idea is culled mostly from Grierson's comments although, in a letter to Grierson in August, 1953 on the occasion of arranging a showing of *Man of Africa* to Tallents and Walter Elliott, Balcon wrote:

> I suppose you and I really always had the same idea that we would like to make five or six pictures a year of *The Brave Don't Cry* or *Song of Africa* type. This is something I have always had in mind for Group 3. To compete in the ordinary feature field is something I would have very little interest in.[11]

John Baxter, director of numerous films combining realist and fictional elements, was involved as well. As production controller, he helped, according to Mr. Hardy, "on behalf of the independent producers, to formulate the case for the National Film Finance Corporation."[12] Group 3 started with a staff of technicians (there were twenty-nine in 1953) and a story department under Stella Jonckheere. It was a permanent film-production company. Grierson described it this way:

> Group 3 took over the Southall Studio and started work in 1951. It assembled an excellent team of craftsmen and in this matter made a contribution, notable at the time, to the

general problem of unemployment in the industry. It set up a modest staff for production control at Civil Service salaries and, in certain aspects, proposed to continue the Government documentary film tradition making films on as modest terms as possible.[13]

Between 1951 and 1955, Group 3 produced twenty-two small-scale productions on a continuous basis, "throwing," according to Grierson, "all artificial and adventitious charges out of our budgets"[14]—in short, they used twenty-five percent of a normal feature-film budget. The use of regional story settings, which lent themselves to projecting the physical aspects of Britain, helped to keep the budgets down. Some of the films showed great seriousness — notably *The Brave Don't Cry* and *Man of Africa*. Most, however, were comedies à la Ealing or films investigating a small family drama. The first film made, *Judgment Deferred*, a thriller directed by John Baxter, ironically, set the tone for Group 3. The script was available and the studio and technicians were ready to go. Long-term strategies were difficult to formulate under those production pressures, and Group 3 was never free of them.

The film that made the most money was co-produced with Countryman Films: *Everest* was a documentary on Hillary and Tenzing's conquering of that mountain. Many directors like John Taylor (*Everest*), Philip Leacock (*The Brave Don't Cry*), Terry Bishop, and John Eldridge, had come up through the documentary. Others had formation in fiction production only. Grierson himself did not direct in this series, but he produced nine of the films, spending his energies especially on *Man of Africa, Devil on Horseback*, and the heralded *The Brave Don't Cry*.

Like every other film genre, the documentary has its system of codes on which is based its "reality." *The Brave Don't Cry* is an interesting study of how documentary codes have been used in fiction to suggest "actuality." "Realism" is, of course, a difficult, complex, and elusive term. What is realistic for one audience in one time and place does not necessarily hold true for another. What is realistic in a western film cannot be transferred to a melodrama or a documentary.

Grierson's attitude to reality in cinema is heavily influenced by Flaherty's work, which is the expression of man's nobility when facing a hostile environment. Although Grierson, in opposition to Flaherty, would stay within the industrial working environment, he also sought a poetic cinema that would ennoble man; according to Grierson, "God will always bring beauty to the edifice of truth."[15]

Grierson's principles of documentary — the cinema's capacity for getting around, for observing and selecting from life itself, the use of the original or native actor and/or scene rather than the studio, and the materials and stories from the raw—add up to an idea of how to make cinema more relevant, closer to the audience's experiences, a rejection of old codes of realism (studio-bound, scripted narratives), concentration on the pro-filmic event, and the dominance of the observation of the camera rather than of the editing or the scripting. *The Brave Don't Cry*, a scripted, narrative fiction film, is an imitation of these codes of Griersonian documentary realism.

First, we have the dominance of what is observable; the film evolves around what can be seen by the camera eye and the eye of the operator as he moves. That is, there are no strangely angled shots (from the heel of a foot, à la Eisenstein); nor are there shots set in montage suggesting memory or feelings. Rather, the images are those which follow events as they unfold in the physical locality as seen by an observer. Nor does the camera walk in by itself, observing, eavesdropping, slipping around corners, or coming down from above to catch life unawares. No, each image is an image seen by others, a public image, authentic because it is witnessed. There are two exceptions: when Mrs. Wishart cries at the kitchen table after hearing the news of the cave-in, and later when she exits from the mining office, confirmed in her fears. These two exceptions are the most moving moments in the film.

In documentary realism, the camera could not go where the men are trapped. Here, the problem of maintaining that realism is dealt with in two ways. First, the camera does not go to the smaller group of trapped men, which includes Dan Wishart; ultimately not rescued, they are presumed dead. The camera does go, however, to the larger group of trapped men — later to be rescued — but only after contact via the telephone. Given the primacy of the spoken word in *The Brave Don't Cry*, and its authority to carry much of the narrative information, this deviation is not perceived as such.

Although the interior of the mine, where the trapped men wait, is a studio set, the shooting is done as if the camera were confined in a narrow space. (Many documentaries are shot partially on sets to maintain authenticity of place. A good example is the inside of the train's sorting car in *Night Mail*.) The primacy of the word affects every aspect of *The Brave Don't Cry*. It is the word, the speech that controls the editing, that carries the film forward in its narrative. This is connected intimately with the earlier observation that the camera is not a free, observing agent but the eye of a human going only where invited. It is the action of the characters — consoling, conveying information, waiting for response, demanding information. It is that pushing for and towards verbal communication that impels the camera eye, the image to this or that point. That image of Mrs. Wishart, alone, crying at the table, exists only because, a moment before, we heard bad news reported to her.

We have here the authenticity of spoken language, conventions of regional speech reflected in the idioms, the dialect, and the rhythms. This authenticity of speech, of communication, is strengthened by the repetition, by information being heard by one party, then carried to another party. The authenticity of that town, of that movement and energy to convey clear information, to make clear, to connect the rescuers with the miners and with the wives means that speech expands in this film to fill every crevice — it is speech repeated, carried carefully and fully so that the audience hears and sees. Is it a carry-over from the lack of verbal ellipsis that the film has so few visual ellipses? The concentration on observed speech means that we are not getting cinematic codes of passage of time, or at least, though we know time is passing, and has passed, we don't know how much. The screen is filled with images of speech and, because the visuals follow the elaborated speech so faithfully and conscientiously, there is little room for symbolic imagery.

The Brave Don't Cry is more documentary than a documentary: the opening shots of smoke and rain seem only to mean smoke and rain; that is we can draw only narrow conclusions: that the mine is working, that the rain, as we see, collapses the ground, causing the mine's cave-in. It is remarkable that neither of these images are given any overt symbolic or poetic power. Things are what they are. Or are they? The more uncontrolled an image, the more it presents itself as unproblematic, the more the reader is forced to try to make connections. In *The Brave Don't Cry* the image of the rain and, later, the image of the woman crying at the table are linked. Or rather we feel they should be linked, that the relationship should have been made, but it was not. But ah, we say, of course, this is a documentary; nature does not, in real life, cry out for man's great pain as it does in Shakespeare.

The concentration on what is authentically observable, the characters in the landscape, is common in Griersonian documentary. The viewer is presented with a middle ground — there is neither intense character development nor an examination of the social-political structure. One aspect of this middle ground unfolding in its narrative is that we perceive it as "natural." Seeing, presumably, is understanding. When a woman sits crying at the table, she is anxious for the safety of her husband. While the complexity of her thoughts and feelings are hidden from us, we feel that we understand what is going on. But how does that work?

First, we understand it through the stereotyped concepts of people — men and women: women must wait, while brave men and boys don't cry. No new ground is broken here, either in the expression of feelings, or in the characterization of people; indeed, if the characters were not stereotypical, we would be at sea.

Secondly, the understanding comes from the contemporary projection on the screen of how people behave in wartime: stoically, bravely, honourably. *The Brave Don't Cry* is a propaganda film about fighting back. It's meant to be uplifting — man has survived! Well, old Dan is gone, but his widow passed on information vital to the rescue. (By the way, why is it, when Mrs. Wishart remembers where Dan had placed the water-pipe and revealed exactly where the men are, that others say "Old Dan had a good memory"? What about Mrs. Wishart's memory?) The film is strongly reminiscent of wartime films, not only in setting and situation (not work, but danger), but in men's and women's separation, fear of death and explosions, the use of gas masks, the singing under stress, the revolt among men, the growing need and understanding of discipline, the pecking order of men and women, and the need to pull together with the women having to wait while the men are in the fore of the battle. The audience's knowledge and recognition of these relationships and loyalties could be taken for granted by the film-makers in 1951-52.

Finally, this film gets its authority from the reputation of the film-makers, especially Grierson, whose involvement with the subject enhanced its social significance and prestige. Responses to a film are not, after all, contained wholly on the screen, but are influenced by the reputations of the "stars."

The film falls into the Griersonian tradition in being politically conservative. Mrs. Wishart tells the young woman (in order to establish a wiser and more experienced character) that she has seen this all "many times before." The young lady demands to know how many times, but no answer is forthcoming. How many times has it happened? Who is responsible? (Surely not the rain.) Nevertheless, the disaster is treated as a natural one. Where are the mine owners? People would ask all these questions in the interest of the working class. Why was this historical disaster turned into a hermetically sealed, sociological study of a community under pressure from, literally and figuratively, within?

Although I have not seen *Man of Africa* or *Devil on Horseback* I will talk about Grierson's important relationship with them as gleaned through his correspondence. *Man of Africa* originated by way of the Colonial office.

Directed by Cyril Frankel and produced by John Grierson, *Man of Africa* set out to be documentary in tone. It was shot in Uganda using native, non-professional actors. Sets had to be built to conform with the written script, and some script ideas had to be amended to fit in with available locations. The Ugandan government was concerned about being ridiculed or not being given proper credit for the Resettlement Scheme, which motivates the film's action. Back in England, Grierson made the necessary reassurances, while insisting on an all-black story. In a letter to Frankel, Grierson writes:

> I think there is every assurance that the beginning of the film will give the reason for the resettlement.... You must, at all costs, avoid any undertaking that you will show the "government organization behind." It has been the weakness of all African films that too much stress was laid on the white element. Your way is the wisest one and indeed it would be better to suggest the white man's magic than to articulate it. I do not feel obliged at all to articulate the government's resettlement scheme in the film itself. This is not a propaganda film, or presumably Sir Andrew Cohen would be paying for it. On the other hand, there can be no question we would wish to give the most generous credits to the Uganda government in our titles and I am writing Sir Andrew Cohen, through the Colonial office, to this effect.[16]

24

Grierson's continuing interest and ability to deal with governments in a compromising manner is expressed here. More importantly, justification is made, in the name of cinema, not to deal with political issues, but to concentrate, "documentary-style," on what can be *observed*.

After first viewings, many people involved in Group 3, including Balcon, Lawrie, and Frankel himself, commented that the story lacked narrative coherence. Balcon wrote to Grierson on 1 September, 1953: "Too many threads are started, are only sketched in and lack proper story-telling and emphasis, and clarification as to both story-line and theme does not emerge until too late."[17] Later in a Montreal interview, Grierson referred to that problem: "Our directors were very good. . . . The odd thing was that we failed and here was my failure: I missed the boat on the writers."[18] In order to solve the narrative problem in *Man of Africa*, a further documentary ploy was used. Narration was introduced to give background to the characters, to help bridge faulty dialogue and to disclaim the film's fictional status by announcing that "there are no actors in this picture, that the people in the film are the Ugandan people themselves and that the incidents in the story are based on fact." Frankel commented: "At present we give the impression that the cast is composed of African actors. This I feel detracts from the nature of the picture."[19]

As far as I can see *Man of Africa* had no chance of success. The crew went in to shoot a fiction film using the documentary style of *The Brave Don't Cry*, but without the aid of professional actors and without knowing their subject. If they had gone to shoot a documentary, they would have, like Flaherty, spent months or years with the natives. The camera eye doesn't by itself see the smooth, worn surfaces of life; the cameraman must recognize them. *Man of Africa* wasn't meant to work as fiction, and it couldn't work as documentary drama. It was cut from ninety minutes to seventy-four minutes for the Edinburgh Film Festival in 1954. Further chopping reduced it to a forty-four-minute travelogue. During its editing, discussion, and re-editing, Grierson was either in hospital, or at home, recovering from tuberculosis.

This was also true for the whole shooting of *Devil on Horseback*, directed by Cyril Frankel and produced by Grierson and Isobel Pargiter. Because of Grierson's illness, there was a furious exchange of letters, most specifically over the question of the

25

script. Stuart Legg was hired just before shooting as on-the-spot producer, but resigned shortly afterwards over the issue of a muddled script. The shooting script, to which Grierson had agreed with minor changes, had become a script without clout:

> The picture was about the troubles of genius. It is not clearly about this anymore. The issue about the short pull is lost. I am bound to say too that some of the depth has gone out of the story. It does not seem as significant as it was. The poetic note which it struck is much diminished. So are the humours.[20]

In nine long, exquisite pages, Grierson completely analyzed the characterizations, aspects of hierarchic tradition, and the traditional discipline of a jockey-training establishment as befits the theme. The thoroughness and clarity of Grierson's analysis and his expressed disappointment in the story's construction point sharply to his own successful training within the Group 3 format; that is, he understood the intimate and subtle relationship between the reality of the world of horse flesh and the demands of character and narrative development. He ended his analysis on a private and pessimistic note:

> It was one thing to clip the wings of Scarlett: I would have done it myself. It is another to cut the wings *off* him. The danger is, lest we have cut the wings off the film itself.

Group 3 has been dismissed as a failure by most critics; nor has its failure often been given more than a short paragraph to finish off a discussion of the terrible fifties in British cinema. But failure is of consequence and it demands analysis. Group 3 should have succeeded: it embodied the strengths of British cinema and in its avowed programme, pointed to the strengths needed for its survival. In the first category of embodied strengths, I put Grierson and Balcon, leaders in the documentary and fiction fields. Their ability to create enthusiastic and loyal units, to train and nurture film-makers, to produce well and cheaply, had been proven. Both were imaginative, experimental producers with a desire to produce an authentically national cinema.

In its programme, Group 3's training of young talent was most important. Like the training grounds of the EMB, the GPO, and the

NFB, training at Group 3 was subject to production level. In good times, many people can learn; in times of cutbacks, training is hard to come by. Small countries with healthy national cinemas have national film schools — Poland, Cuba, Australia. While there are links between the training and production in those countries they are not as devastatingly intimate as they were and are in the British and Canadian units mentioned. I would like to hear comment on this during our discussion.

Group 3 vowed to carve out a position for independent producers. The source of the collapse exists here. Group 3 was always dependent on the distributors, in short, there was no production, there *is* no production, independent of distributor control. Otherwise, you just can't make your money back. Grierson railed against the critics, at the time, for not assisting Group 3 with "constructive critical aid," as they had done for documentary. Unfortunately, Grierson was ill, and Balcon was preoccupied with running Ealing Studios. Nevertheless, the films they made, at such-and-such speed and at such-and-such costs, had everything to do with available distribution. The other two groups — Rank and ABCP—that received money from NFFC to recover could now, after three years, take fresh risks in the production field. Grierson remarked that "what perhaps the successes of Group A and Group B conceal was the fact that they looked after only the relatively established big picture men among the independents and only of a proportion of these."

So, as the big boys got healthier, they protested against the continued support by the NFFC of Group 3. These protestors were the same distributors who put Group 3 films in the lower half of double bills so that the films earned a flat fee and not a percentage of the box office. The death knell of Group 3 was sounded by the new director of the NFFC:

> Unfortunately Group 3 has had considerable financial trouble and the Board has now decided to abandon its policy of continuous production. It is difficult enough for any production organization to maintain a continuous program. It is particularly difficult for Group 3, being dependent on new talent. It is now apparent that the type of middle-budget picture which is most appropriate for the training of new directors is not suited to the present pattern of exhibitors.[21]

27

[1] John Grierson, "Definitions — Answers to a Cambridge Questionnaire," in *John Grierson: Film Master*, James Beveridge (New York: Macmillan, 1978), pp. 343-44.

[2] Forsyth Hardy, *John Grierson: A Documentary Biography* (London: Faber and Faber, 1979), p. 169.

[3] Annette Kuhn, "'Independent' Film-making and the State in the 1930s," *Edinburgh '77 Magazine No. 2: History/Production/Memory*, p. 47.

[4] Hardy, p. 169.

[5] Harry Watt, *Don't Look at the Camera* (London: Paul Elek, 1975), p. 186.

[6] Charles Barr, "'Projecting Britain and the British Character': Ealing Studios," *Screen*, 15, No. 1. (Spring 1974), p. 96.

[7] Barr, p. 97.

[8] Roy Armes, *A Critical History of British Cinema* (London: Secker & Warburg, 1978), p. 180.

[9] Armes, p. 189.

[10] Armes, p. 189.

[11] Letter from Sir Michael Balcon to John Grierson (London, August 17, 1953): The John Grierson Archive, University of Stirling #6:36:208.

[12] Hardy, p. 181.

[13] John Grierson's history and statement of Group 3 (Circa 1955), 15 pages typewritten and corrected by hand: The John Grierson Archive, University of Stirling, p. 5.

[14] John Grierson, "On Group 3," *Sight and Sound* (Jan.-March 1952), p. 103.

[15] As spoken in his lecture at McGill, 1969.

[16] Letter from John Grierson to Cyril Frankel (London, March 3, 1952): The John Grierson Archive, University of Stirling #6:35:12.

[17] Letter from Sir Michael Balcon to John Grierson (London, September 1, 1953): The John Grierson Archive, University of Stirling #6:36:288.

[18] John Grierson, interviewed by Les Nirenberg, C.B.C. (Montreal, April 2, 1969).

[19] Letter from Cyril Frankel to John Grierson, John Baxter and Isobel Pargiter (September 2, 1953): The John Grierson Archive, University of Stirling #6:36:231.

[20] Letter from John Grierson to John Baxter (Calstone, June 23, 1953): The John Grierson Archive, University of Stirling #6:36:122.

[21] Address delivered by Mr. D. Kingsley to the Association of Ciné Technicians, (March 6, 1955): The John Grierson Archive, University of Stirling #6:1:3.

JAMES BEVERIDGE

Grierson and Distribution

DISTRIBUTION has been mentioned a number of times today. Most of the film people here, however, come from the production side. The true rôle of distribution has never been evaluated adequately. There is a theme we can discover in this. We heard a discussion on the circumstances of Grierson's arrival, who brought him from the other side, and how it came about. My proposition is that the time in Canada was ripe for Grierson's idea.

The situation in Canada in the late 1930s was indeed favourable to the arrival of an idealist, a propagandist. Now, we Canadians have our own sense of development in Canada. We see ourselves as either a young, an aging, or a graciously middle-aged nation, depending where we stand in the spectrum. We have our own memories and recollections of growing up in this country, how it was in the thirties, how it was in the fifties, and how it is today. In this country, latterly, there has been a huge surge of growth and dynamism, development and high tech, immigration and prosperity, all contributing to patterns of credit and affluence. In short, we are enjoying, with some exuberance, elevated standards of living. We live in the First World, we are among the top ten, rich and fat, even though things may look shaky. Nonetheless, we are in this happy, affluent position.

In 1935 to 1940, it was not so. We remember the rigorous and rather grisly years of the Great Depression, the miseries of the West, unemployment, the loss of homes, the drought, and so on. A pattern of hardships, unemployment, and general distress existed in the cities and in the rural world of Canada. Nonetheless, all was not bare and sterile. There were some agencies and individuals who had a brighter vision and solid confidence that things would develop, that we would make it. But that required a definition of our rôle, our autonomy, our expectations, of our relationships with Britain, the "mother country," and with the great overwhelming neighbour always breathing hot breath at us from the south. There was the problem of our own internal stresses.

Canada was never a simple country. But there were people here, when Grierson was brought here, already working actively in the arts, politics, social development, and communication. They were concerned with Canada, and they had ambitions and aspirations for Canada: poets, literary figures, painters, musicians, political thinkers, and writers. We were not starved for talent, nor for creative and productive output. The National Film Society movement was a specific instance, and it began, against adversity, in the middle thirties.

Donald Buchanan's name is associated with the cultural infrastructure and patient knitting up of this pattern, as are many other names. The Crawleys were interested parties. Alan and Bobby Plaunt of Ottawa were interested. They, too, became film enthusiasts. As happens in every society, the natural-born enthusiasts gravitate with ardent affection and interest towards the place where the action is, the exhibition, study, and pursuit of films. They, in part, were responsible for Grierson coming.

Ross McLean, who succeeded Grierson, and Donald Buchanan were prime movers of the Film Society movement. Ross McLean, who was working in London, proposed to the high commissioner, Vincent Massey, that Canadians adopt a documentary pattern like that evident in Britain. McLean and Buchanan believed that Canada should be active in the film-society movement and in documentary film-making. Vincent Massey, a man of culture and refinement, was amenable to this proposition. The proposition put to the government was that Grierson be brought to consider and prepare some kind of film legislation, and some general plan for the utilization of film. All this happened before the war, roughly 1938.

Grierson had been here before. Despite Forsyth Hardy's detailed descriptions of Grierson's visits, there's still some degree of vagueness about the number of them, the exact extent, and his exact itinerary. If Evelyn Spice Cherry were here, she could perhaps inform us a bit further. The British were concerned about the Canadian loyalties at a time when the prospect of a war was looming; perhaps it's not too blunt to put it that way. In the twenties, studies were done by British delegates who came here and examined the situation.

These delegates professed alarm at the extent to which American films were flooding into Canada. Hardly any indigenous Canadian production or feature films existed. They felt we were being snow-balled or storm-tossed, and generally overwhelmed by the Americans who, of course, captured our market sixty years ago and never let it go. Famous Players, which is essentially Paramount, had been the dominant film exhibitor in Canada.

So there was concern in Britain that the loyalties of this dominion might become tinctured, adulterated, or loosened. This American influence would stimulate support from the British side for any effort on the Canadian side to develop indigenous Canadian-made and Canadian-based films. The British government could see the crisis ahead, and they needed to be reassured of the loyalties of Canada, the willingness and readiness to be counted. Canada was, after all, the senior loyal dominion. There was, therefore, a general interest on both sides. A film development here would help Canadians cohese and cohere, and palpitate with loyalty and constancy. So Grierson was brought here.

Part of the story, the part with which we're most familiar, is the creation of the film-making instrument. Many of you here today came with that first wave of wet-behind-the-ears enthusiasm, whether from journalism, school-teaching, commercial art, or whatever field. We had the great privilege and joy of working, in those early years, with Grierson, Stuart Legg, Stanley Hawes, and with many distinguished visitors, such as Boris Kaufmann.

Boris was Dziga Vertov's brother, and he came as a refugee cameraman from the French industry to work with us briefly. Joris Ivens came, Robert Flaherty dropped in and dropped out again. There was always a sense, even in our locally based, Ottawa-based existence in the John Street saw-mill, of the international community of film people and film outlets, and also, apart from the film-making, of the application and use of films.

My contention is that Canadians should pay attention to, and examine more broadly, the historical situation and the mood, the talents and the operational elements, the audible Canadian voices at that time, 1938, 1939. I'm indebted to Geoff Andrew, a seasoned veteran of those years, with much personal experience, for his interpretation of this period. I've talked also to Roby Kidd in Ottawa. He was associated in some measure with this development, too. Graham Spry was another ardent Canadian with aspirations and beliefs in Canadian development.

Leaving aside the film-making, an apparatus was formed for communicating throughout this sprawling country. Some of its elements were not formally structured. It consisted of a grass-roots, warp-and-woof process, a weaving and knitting-up, an exploitation and utilization of existing available agencies. The interests and talents of many ardent, sometimes slightly nutty individuals stood ready to be fired up either by Grierson in person, or by his ideas.

Meeting Grierson or talking to his close colleagues was an energizing experience. His staff's loyalty and their understanding of his intentions and motives provided a wonderful process of filtration, personal communication. It's a bit difficult to see how it worked. Most of us here have some specific association with Grierson. Essentially the whole process is a jigsaw, a fragmented picture. It's hard to define the overview — the production and distribution sides of making films and other information materials; the political, commercial, aesthetic, and philosophical sides, the bilingual side, the situation of Canadians vis-à-vis Britain, and the aspirations of Canadians to be truly independent.

Let us look now at some of the agencies in this process. I've drawn a primitive visual aid here on the blackboard, which will give an idea of the existing patterns and agencies in Canada that were utilized by Grierson. To a degree, they have remained as active elements. Some of them have been overtaken, or replaced by newer agencies in our contemporary Canada.

Let us start in the middle of the diagrams: "films," by which we mean film-making and film-using; and "WIB," which is the Wartime Information Board. The WIB was a structure that began a two-part operation most effectively in its largest phase of activity at the beginning of 1943. It had, by designation, large powers to project morale-building and information-disseminating policies throughout the Canadian state. How would it do that? Well, from 1938 through to 1941, the early phase of the war, there were the following inter-relating elements.

There was the film industry — perhaps the untidiest or the most raffish. It is essential, if you're carrying a message to the broad public audience, to reach the cinemas and movie theatres with their plush seats, brass rails, and double features. Grierson, by devious and unconventional means, together with his colleagues and advisors, obtained contracts and deals with Columbia Pictures in Canada and United Artists in the United States and Canada. For the first time, Canadians were able to persuade the American motion-picture industry to allow the Canadian some profit-making in Canada, and even in the United States, as part of Canada's war effort. The civil establishment was taking on new duties, preparing, contributing, working for the cause.

In the international sense, a perspective was appearing, not only for now but for beyond the war. Few people were looking beyond the war in 1943, because the prospect was dark. But Grierson, Legg, and an informal circle of advisors were looking to the future. Grierson subscribed certainly to futurist opinions, other expertise, and perspectives. As Professor Lockerbie has said, his mind was open to many areas, and to many models and spokesmen of policy and philosophy. His "World in Action" vehicle, a theatrical short-film series, twenty minutes, was related to the *March of Time*. It was a bit derivative. It used Lorne Green's stentorian, doomful voice, but the perspective was international. That was one element that brought down a certain suspicion of Grierson and Legg, an uncertainty concerning their exact focus and motive, and their ideology in conceiving and circulating international films such as the "World in Action" series.

At this time, the CBC radio was another large factor in Canadian life. It had shown great development and achievement in its radio skills, including writing, reporting, public affairs, drama, and adult education. This educational element was strong in Canadian life; it must be the Scots influence. The CBC was powerful, intent on co-ordinating and bringing together all the elements of the Canadian community, whatever their origin or employment. It strove for a common understanding, and looked to a better future, one more richly productive than the recent past had been. The CBC had two particularly influential features: the "Farm Forum" and the "Citizens Forum." Our population in 1939 was still largely rural; now it's overwhelmingly urban. "Farm Forum," reaching into all the farm patterns in Canada, in all the provinces, was a valuable and precise instrument of information. It communicated and educated, and was used to co-ordinate information with other programs and agencies for wartime objectives. As for the "Citizens Forum" on public affairs, the CBC has always been strong in public affairs, and continues to be so. Even today, public affairs remains dominant in our national radio and television. We hear from our friends and associates in the United States, for example, how keenly they miss the CBC. So, the CBC was then and is now a powerful editorial voice. It should logically be the Film Board's natural ally, but there has been a lamentable lack of mutual connubial enthusiasm between the two. They worked, nevertheless, as natural allies in the general spreading of information concerned with major themes and editorial considerations.

The "Rural Circuits," evolved by and within the Film Board itself, was a distribution pattern within the provinces involving the active participatory support and collaboration of the university-extension departments. The Film Board, in collaboration with the universities, designed programs of films to publicize common themes, policies, and causes. This first large-scale distribution pattern for sixteen-mm films shown outside the cinemas was developed by the Board's Donald Buchanan, prime architect of the plan. Not only was the plan important: it worked as an activist organizer within the intra-agency field.

The universities that contributed and were principally involved included the universities of British Columbia, Alberta, Manitoba, Prince Edward Island, New Brunswick, and Laval. (Grierson had a continuing relationship with Social Sciences Dean Levesque at Laval. The connection is important to note in view of Grierson's concern with the Film Board's policy in French film-making: a complex and highly interesting Canadian question.) This relationship between Grierson and Levesque probably occurred because, at that time, there was the beginning in Quebec of a loosening-up process, a loosening of clerical control over various social elements and organizations. That's a field for more study and precise investigation.

The university-extension departments helped to organize travelling film circuits, each with a presenter or supervisor. These supervisors, trained in rigorously designed study sessions, either at Banff or Macdonald College, were, in fact, field travelling projectionists. They not only ran the show, they led discussion afterwards to prompt opinions, synthesize points of view, and report the results. They connected the field and the centre. This was a very significant and important development in communications practice. It ended because of finances, but during the war years and for a period after, this system of rural circuits exhibited films effectively in many country areas. The itinerant projectionists worked "on the beat" and maintained an information program of value in collaboration with the universities.

Labour was another broad sector. The trade-union film-circuits were instigated and planned in the same way as the circuits for rural distribution. Major unions were approached and their leaders consulted. The unions, of course, supported the war effort with energy. They supported the work of the WIB, too, the broad national programs of information, not only through their unions' memberships but through other related community agencies. Among the churches, the United and the Presbyterian were willing and supportive towards this information activity. The Church of England was cooler.

There were, in addition, some important Ottawa-based agencies who played a significant part in these national programs, such as the Canadian Council for Education through Citizenship which, as I understand it, was a co-ordinating body willing to give its good offices in Ottawa to make contacts and to help bring together like-minded people in various agencies. The Canadian Education Association represented schools, teachers, and professional associations. The Canada Foundation helped to set up and fund the dissemination of films and information materials to the armed services. The purpose was to reach the servicemen so that they, too, had an inflow of information on what was happening, what the country was doing towards the war effort, and what were the prospects for a more hopeful future after the war.

So Ottawa, that not-very-big capital, still sponsored a community of national interest and sympathy in support of these objectives. People became more aware, and the programs effected a kind of grouping, a relationship between these like-minded and positive-minded elements. Not to dwell too long on this, I'd like to mention two particular training centres — the Banff School of Fine Arts, which represented the extension activity of Alberta and was used for annual workshop sessions, and Macdonald College at Ste Anne de Bellevue, that leading agricultural college, advisor on agricultural policy and research.

In this context also, public libraries come to mind; they are a kind of community centre in themselves. The libraries became prime vehicles for film distribution in the years after the war, in addition to their original rôles as book and study centres. The libraries reach special-interest groups, have systems of circulation, filing, classification for reference, and borrowing. They provide a central meeting place, and can put on shows of specialized and functional value. The Canadian Association for Adult Education was, and is, perhaps, the prime agency in this whole support structure. Ned Corbett, then director, was a great promoter and believer in the national causes. According to one view, it was he who nominated Grierson as operational head of film activities set up under the Film Board. In any case, there was a collaboration, and the Canadian Association for Adult Education continues to regard adult education as a prime social need and function in our national life.

Men of fine calibre were recruited for the design of training programs and film-circuit operations. There were Film Board stalwarts such as Len Chatwin of Vancouver, Charley Marshall of Victoria, Dooley Grey of Alberta, Vaughan Deacon, a feisty militant of Toronto, and many others. They were the grass-roots believers, intelligent, earnest, and vigorous. A very large part of this development must be credited to their work. It was untiring, and of very high quality.

This then, in bare outline, is my proposition — that Grierson did not create the world in six days. But, when he came, because of his own interests, his dynamism, his philosophical principles and beliefs, he was able to make contact. He made connections on both sides of the water, and they worked. There were stresses and strains, of course, and plenty of fights. The conduct, policy, and operations of the Wartime Information Board were not wholly peaceful, but the pattern was indeed a national program. Grierson, in a short time, was assigned responsibilities of a very large order, not only for designing and shaping editorial and philosophical guidelines for the country, but for effecting, through the educational agencies and elements in all provinces, those means and methods through which the guidelines could be communicated.

It was an extraordinary period in Canadian life and in the practice of national communications. It was not a dictatorship or a military junta. It was essentially a Canadian pattern. When Grierson came, the time was ripe for it. The crisis of the war and its terrible strains and sufferings were there. No doubt the war brought an infusion of adrenalin into the national bloodstream, which fortified and strengthened this pulse of activity, dedication to work, production, and common cause. The films, both political and unpretentious, many of which had nothing directly to do with the war effort, looked to the future; these films reflected a richer, more cultural, intellectual side of Canada that was fast developing.

During the period, a new generation of film-makers came blundering along and, gradually, film by film, disaster by disaster, they learned the way, shaped their talents and skills, and produced some very fine material in many cases. Many of these early films have survived the test of time. The researchers of tomorrow will understand their images and symbols. So this distinctive and specific pattern of expression evolved, and we should perhaps give attention to this specific time in Canada, to the development of what have become major cultural thrusts and ideas and operational principles in our national life. It was a vital and fruitful time, maybe divinely touched by Grierson's arrival on the scene.

Beveridge: [in answer to a question about the Bureau] The Canadian Motion Picture Bureau played a minor part, but not at all negligible. There was a long-established film-making plant in Ottawa. It was a means of production; maybe it was pretty rinky-dink, almost pre-industrial, in 1940. They did tourist films for many years, as Lady Elton says, *Where the Moose Runs Loose, A Literary Fish Story, Canoe Trails Through Mooseland*. Those pictures, however, went all over the commonwealth and piled up, in what must be embarrassing quantities, at the Imperial Institute in London, where they were shown to generations of defenceless school-children. The Canadian governments, predisposed to high-tech, had used films for immigration purposes and tourist promotion since early years — in Ontario since 1912, depicting the joys of rural farm life for the intending immigrants from Yorkshire. It's a strange and long-standing precedent. The Motion Picture Bureau was absorbed, through the pressure of events, into the Film Board which, at the start, had no equipment — one typewriter, one secretary, one paper clip, and an office in the West Block. The Film Board started production in this hay-wire saw-mill on the Rideau River, but the technical means were there. They were adequate.

Badgley was an honourable man who had carried on the maintenance of a film unit at the Motion Picture Bureau in the dire depression years. He protected with great loyalty this staff of returned men from World War I who, in the 1920s and thirties, made these silent tourist pictures on tinted green-and-purple film stock, for purposes of tourism and immigration. The Bureau had a rôle, and some functional value. Badgley was caught up and absorbed into the Film Board machinery, and was not reconciled or happy with that fate. He left in some bitterness, a casualty of the development process.

Elspeth Chilsholm: How about Grierson's relations with the press?

Beveridge: I can't go too far in that because I'm not well-enough acquainted with the ground. Much of it has to do with the west, the great tradition of the *Free Press*. Dafoe was, at that time, of course, at the end of his career, and Grierson's great friend George Ferguson takes over the *Free Press*. There is a very good friend in Charles Woodsworth of the Southam Press in Ottawa, and there were other individual editorial writers and journalists throughout the country — men like Jack Scott of the Vancouver *Sun*. There was a community of people. Some of you here might know who they were.

Colin Low: You mentioned Donald Buchanan — his family ran the Lethbridge *Herald*.

Beveridge: Yes, that's the kind of connection that was made. There are many. Look how many Scotsmen there are in the cast of characters.

Geoff Andrew: I'd just like to say one thing: that's a good description of the Grierson web from the time that his responsibilities expanded beyond the film area into the Wartime Information Board. He was, in fact, responsible for a larger area than we know. He always talked about Canadian society, and he was very fortunate to have, as a native-born Canadian partner, Ned Corbett of the CAAE. Corbett had great influence with the CBC's Talks Division, which was, at that time, the ablest group of women running Neil Morrison, that Canada ever produced. That whole web disappeared after the era of Grierson and Corbett. The co-operation that had kept all these people working together subsided. The CBC became so professional it didn't need any advice from the public, and something of the same, I think, happened to the Film Board. Grierson, however, had his tentacles out everywhere and, from the year 1943 — his influence must have lasted through to 1946 and 1947 — and then it sort of subsided. We didn't have either Grierson or Corbett any longer.

I just want to correct you on one thing. The Canada Foundation was a creation of Walter Herbert's, along with Herb Lash, from the early Film Board days. He started this cultural foundation, and Grierson and the rest of us in the Film Board, or rather the Wartime Information Board, used it, and the films, to culturally infiltrate the occupying army of the American soldiery who were up in the north creating the Alaska Highway and the airfields, in order to move aircraft to the Russians. As a matter of fact, the Americans were fine up there, and they did a wonderful job. We just wanted to remind them that this was another country, and that there were some cultural opportunities to learn about Canada through communications and film, through publications, and so on. The important thing was that Walter Herbert's little organization got a temporary infusion of money to create this cultural objective. But the whole thing, Jim, I think, needs thorough research because, if we think of Grierson only in terms of film, we miss the man's range and his effect.

Beveridge: There is one thing in all of this that is implicit, and it's the conflict or tension between centralism and the grass-roots. There is a centralist policy in any emergency, in a sense like the War Measures Act, special powers that would normally, in ordinary times, be contested. In wartime, there is a felt urgency for centralism. It's built up on the basis of grass-roots structures by local people with their own autonomy, status, and contacts. Now, at this moment, Mr. Lou Applebaum is in the best position to speak knowledgeably. There is much confusion now of our potential, with satellites, cables, pay-TV, with the proliferation of channels, the perfect inundation of the citizen by waves of solicited and unsolicited video, television, all that coloured slush with a modicum of very high-calibre intellectual, educational content. Our problem is how to filter, sift, schedule, whether and how to regulate the input. This is the nightmare, to my mind. Louis Applebaum and his colleagues have been hearing representations from every body of interest in Canada in the cultural, intellectual, and professional fields, and he knows what confronts us. The great dread, to my mind, is one of anarchy, which could come either through a totally unregulated industry or an excess of centralism and regulation, creating break-away movements, violation, noncooperation, piracy, some kind of unstructured, unregulated free-for-all of unco-ordinated market elements and consumer demands. Perhaps we must look in the present terms for some kind of national pattern, maybe again in terms of such elements as the university-extension services, some activity that is nationally established and effective, but non-bureaucratized by the central government. Agencies that are responsive, simple, flexible, not rigid. Until we have those, and can work with them, I don't see how we can get the feedback, and I do agree that the feedback is of the essence. I think this requires great study and thought. I can't see any pattern at present at all. I don't know if one is there. I think we will have to make some effort to find new groupings, within communities or even municipalities. Who knows? How can we "report back?" We need a collecting agency to adjudicate, evaluate, and consider the material that comes back. Otherwise, how do we know? How can we communicate our feelings nationally? Letters to the press are a pleasant eighteenth-century device. The CBC gets letters — there's a degree of feedback. How extensive is it? In the circumstances of the immediate future, in terms of the proliferation of television systems and cable, there will surely have to be some coherent grid-pattern of concerned, tough-minded people with good causes at heart, to fulfill that kind of evaluating and correlating rôle.

Geoff Andrew: Such an activity will have to be created with an institution. It was created originally by men of passion and imagination, and they held it together as long as their passion and imagination were active in the field. It collapsed after that.

Jim Beveridge: It may need a new movement to regenerate that kind of sentiment among individuals.

Speaker from the floor: Institutions have changed today. There's been a significant shift. You're talking about a different generation and society. It was a very quaint picture in some ways, and I don't mean that as a criticism, but that society is now urbanized and industrialized. The transition has been made. That was Canada forty years ago.

Colin Low: This is very interesting for me because my own background is rural. When I got involved in the project ['Challenge for Change'] at Memorial University, it was their inspiration and their fantastic extension department with twelve community-development, on-location people that helped me. Memorial University is a central university but it is also an adult-education operation. Everything seemed so easy when we did the Fogo Island project. The university stayed responsive to that situation for five years after. Maybe that was the best way to go, because the Film Board couldn't continue to do those experiments. The whole notion of getting other universities and their extension departments to do projects was very exciting, and we tried to transplant it. We worked up an excellent project at the University of Calgary; we did the Drumheller project on video and it looked like it was going to take off. So we tried other universities. I think it was a question of their highly urbanized outlook; they were less concerned with the general problems of their region. They were highly specialized, highly departmentalized, compartmentalized, and it didn't take. We tried it with community colleges. A college out on the west coast did some interesting work, and continues to do so, but we weren't able to transmit the same enthusiasm as at Memorial.

Jim Beveridge: Perhaps a university within a province could initiate and maintain educational programs at different levels by television and cable to an increasing degree, broadening and strengthening its service beyond the local municipality to the region. But how to finance and fund it within the provinces, one doesn't know. All universities are in a crunch, some more than others. A university can achieve a relationship with local districts through television, university-based, if it is done with skill and with a very direct and reciprocal contact with the users, listeners, and viewers. Perhaps there is the possibility of special-interest groups at the receiving end. There may be a whole new field in university programming, in the financing of university-television programming. It seems to me that is something that should be very carefully considered, in the future.

Margaret Ann Elton: Geoff Andrew was talking about the enormous responsibility and dedication of the men behind the task, but it seems now that the advertisers have the licence to speak as educators. They're out for the young market. They have the fashion industry, the pop industry, the pornographic industry. How are we going to find people today with something more than ability and a passion for selling? There's plenty of imagination and passion around, but what are the purposes to which it's directed?

RODRIGUE CHIASSON

The CRTC Tapes

GOOD MORNING. The first reason I am here is to deliver the transcripts of recorded conversations between the late John Grierson and the CRTC from late 1968 to late 1971. There are six hundred and fifty pages of transcripts, and some of the tapes were lost during the frequent moves we had, but most of the conversations were transcribed. Volume Four, and in particular the last part, is incomplete and patchy. It's difficult, but I would say that about ninety percent of the transcripts are true to the original tapes, all of which have been annotated where the inference was obscure, and footnoted and cross-referenced. Much of the content is repetitive, as you might expect from a series of conversations, but I am working on suitable versions for publication. Some two hundred pages have been reorganized thematically. The tapes and conversations can be used for research as they stand. Elspeth Chisholm had asked me to play parts of the tapes but, when I listened to them, the quality sounded poor and unequal. Some of the early ones, taped on the first primitive Philips dictating machine, will be good for those who want to listen closely.

I'd like to say a few words about how all of this came about. I first met with Grierson in December, 1968, shortly after McGill University had asked him to come back to Canada to lecture on mass communications. That was shortly after the creation of the CRTC. I made an appointment to ask him for help in dealing with the media. Grierson's documentary movement was not only work on the documentary film, but a social movement set in motion using films as a means of expression. I knew of his background as a student of philosophy, and as a professor in moral philosophy at the University of Glasgow. The angle of attack I wanted to take with him concerned the ethical aspect of communications for practitioners and agencies like the CRTC, who work in the public sector and influence the public. We wanted him to write, but he no longer wanted to.

R. *Chiasson*: How about conversation?
J. *Grierson*: That's fine.
R. *Chiasson*: How about taping the conversation?
J. *Grierson*: That's fine too.

So that's how we began taping. It was in 1969. The following week, he was in Ottawa. In the beginning, we did one or two hours of taping a week. Towards the end of 1971, we taped when we felt like it, once every two or three weeks, but the conversations were steady and continuous. He came to Ottawa every week and we had conversations in the restaurant, in the office, and at home. André Martin was the director of research at that time; Pierre Juneau was chairman of the CRTC. When we first found out that John Grierson was coming to Canada, we wanted to meet him and learn about his work in Canada. When André Martin was at the *Cahier du Cinema* in France, he met Grierson. The transcripts refer often to criticism; the *Cahier du Cinema* was the review of film criticism and, throughout the conversations, Grierson urges us to create a "Cahier de Télévision." He insisted that we must develop criticism of television.

I was told that this seminar is meant to bring some focus to Grierson's work in Canada. The press releases issued by the organizers mention the obvious, the National Film Board, and well they might; that's his [Grierson's] monument. I shall try to sketch the dimensions of his contribution to the social and political philosophy of action in this country. First, I'll tell you a short story that gives another dimension to the overworked pulpit theme.

I asked him, in the course of our conversations, how deliberately he had set out to nurture and develop the documentary-film movement. He replied, "You'd better believe that it was deliberate, and it wasn't just making films, whatever that is. It was a social movement." That statement takes care of film-making, and lets me off the hook in as much as I don't have to talk shop before the shop itself. It also sets me up for what is the subject of a short talk on Grierson as an efficient exponent and articulator of a social ethic of communication.

It became clear to me from the moment of the first conversation that film, radio, television, the so-called mass media, would serve

43

only as one of the fields for reference to a social ethic of communications. In that first conversation, he referred to Plato's harsh treatment of the poet in the Republic. Before getting into some of the passages of those conversations that illustrate his articulation, in words, of the ethic of public communications, let us consider his articulation, in action, of that ethic, and how he defined inaction of ethics as well as his own ethical position. For the first example, I have chosen the Wartime Information Office, propaganda or counter-propaganda, but propaganda nevertheless. To whom would you entrust that dangerous job other than the obviously brilliant genius whose great track-record had such stars to steer by as the propagation of the faith? He didn't use that [his faith] as an excuse, by the way; he used it seriously, giving hope, the notion that actions of great consequence in the profession of mind-bending (those are his own words) had to be considered *sub spatia*. The phrase means "considered in the light of eternal judgment." Who, having that kind of reference, could stomach the job? Clever men, unburdened with categorical moral imperatives, have taken such jobs and have done what we know. The National Film Board, as an example of definition in action of a social ethic — consider the inspiration he gave to that public-servant's job of making government films that others consider a depressingly creative instinct. He turned it around into a generative principle. Grierson translated duty into horizons, bringing alive visions, moving the population and the politicians to action. He knew that politicians weren't naturally endowed with social vision, and that sort of vision quite often, to quote Rabelais (he liked that quote), comes from below.

Another example was his battle against the free flow of information ideology. Grierson, if he were alive today, would be concerned about the loose talk that goes on about free-flow information, the confusion that quite often is purposely entertained in relation to "free flow" and "freedom of expression." "Free flow" is essentially a spatial thing, and "freedom of expression" an individual thing, or citizen's perogative. He was against free flow because he knew where the flow would come from. His teaching here at McGill was an action of social ethics. The Brechtal attempt to let him speak gives you an idea of his definition in words, not of his ethical position. I remember one morning Grierson coming into my office at the CRTC. We'd been working on charts and papers, trying to identify the characteristics of public versus private communica-

44

tions. He came into my office and said, "You know, I've been thinking about your charts and categories on private communications versus public communications. The fact is, in communications, there is very little that is private: a prayer to God, making love, maybe a confidence; even making love becomes a public thing in a way. There's that marriage licence, you know, so that makes it public." Along the same lines, he once told my daughter, who had shown him one of her paintings, "You know you are in the same class as Michelangelo." He didn't mean that the primitive expression of a thirteen-year-old was Michelangelo quality, but that it had been painted to be shown to a public, however small; to be exposed. In that sense, he was telling that child that her painting was a public communication. The perameters of that, in the sense of his ethics of public communications, can be related to those two statements. First, there is very little in communications that is private; and second, the creative artist is in a field of public communications, and he or she had better remember that the ethical corollaries that flow from that are numerous, the duty of responsibility, the principle of competency, the reference to the public good, and to the public interest.

For Grierson, the correct manner of dealing with every life problem is indicated by the laws of honour of the particular profession to which one belongs and of the particular stage of life that is proper to one's age — for example, Don Quixote's laws of honour become ridiculous in another age. Grierson said, "One is not free to choose; that is, the individual is not free to choose. One belongs to a family, a species, a guild, a craft, a group, a denomination, each one with its own honour and, since this circumstance not only determines to the last degree the regulation for one's private and public conduct, one must honour one's craft. It's not only the medical people who have a Hippocratic oath — I, as a teacher, have a Hippocratic oath that I must not teach chaos to the new generation. They may not go forward, the new generation, with no hope of order." This is a central thing to do. If you're the father of children, you can answer that question with certain things you know by honour of your profession as a father — you are forced to give it — the circumstances not only determine to the last degree the regulation for one's public and private conduct but also represent, according to this, an inclusive and pervasive, unyielding integration.

This process of integration is unyielding because you are a

Canadian, you belong to a profession that makes decisions. Each day you belong to the honorific process of being a parent. Each day you belong to the honorific business of being a public servant. Each day you belong to the honorific business of being a traveller on the road. Every moment you are dealing with this inclusive and pervasive, unyielding process of integration. One may not depart from the rôle one plays. If you are appointed to the rôle of public servant to the public, under the authority of parliament and administerial authority, you can't kid yourself. You can't say *"Vive le Québec libre,"* and you can't pinch money from the Film Board to make any film you please. The real ideal of one's present natural character, one's concern as a judging and acting entity, must be only to meet every life problem in a manner befitting the rôle one plays, whereupon the two aspects of temporal entity, the subjective and the objective, will be joined exactly and the individual be eliminated as a third intrusive factor. He will not then bring into manifestation the temporal accident of his own personality, none of this personality cult.

This honour-bound man was not a simple conservative. He did have conservative traits and he respected conservative thought. He says, "You know, of course, there are other things that affect you, the inspiration of the time, the honour, the honour of your trade as a public servant, as an artist, as a teacher, they are all creative honours. You must see that you are not teaching the same thing every day in your life, because the world is changing." In Grierson's ethic, you can get, in a very complete way, a transitory reading of these. It makes marvellous connections between the dialectic of duty and poetry — it's fascinating. I can't read all the chosen excerpts — it would take too long.

I referred to the Platonic thing at the beginning and he kept warning me, the same warning of the poet, and the republic, and the artist. He was addressing some of the concerns of the Commission. As a regulatory agency and quasi-judicial body, we have to deal with broadcasters, the question of freedom of expression, and the possibility of censorship, where clear and present concerns come through the Commission. His advice was, "When it comes to pictures, don't trust creative men. Only trust creative men when they are also philosopher kings, when they do the Platonic thing." You see, Plato, when he was dealing with the poet of that period, or with the medicine man, was dealing with the fellow who was talking in terms of myth. In another sense, the poet, your creative man, may be a dangerous fellow. The creative people indulged in their personal caprices. The producer's responsibility is exercised as a check and as a creative force. To me, the producer is not just a representative of the treasury: he is a controller on behalf of the public spirit and good; he is also the fellow who can say, "Look here, you stop these confrontations, for God's sake. You're through with that Goddamn thing." When they start confrontations, and you see where it is going to pieces but the producer doesn't spot it, that's important. You're onto something big.

Don't trust the creative fellow. In the same vein, he goes on to interpret, "Don't trust the creative fellow," bringing everything to questions of duty, responsibility, all that sort of thing. We may be talking about something everybody knows, leadership, but what we are talking about also is the management of government, the inspiring of energy, the system by which we create loyalties, the system by which will-power is created, not only in the managerial forces but in the co-operation of people. One of the weaknesses of democratic theory, particularly in America, is that it ducks the pain and dangers of leadership. It's as though we have all these debates in parliament or in congress, with every point of view. We have the Royal Commission, the left, the right, and confrontation. But that's not all. Somebody has to get up and say, "This is a wise policy. This is it."

This brings me to the last example of Grierson's articulation in the words of his social ethic. It's closer to action because, in the course of events, he did not shrink away from specifics. He was in Canada at the time of the War Measures Act and the FLQ crisis, as he had been, indeed, in 1939, during World War Two. Here's what he said, and how he applied his principles to action. Observing on television the proclamation of the War Measures Act and the disputatious interviews on the prime minister's and government's stand, he said, "I am very sorry to see a situation arise in Canada where, since the War Measures Act was enacted, the press, the television, and the media have become disputatious at a time when authority should be absolute. You have the word of your prime minister that it was a situation which was so grave that this action was necessary. You must accept the word of your government, and it's a government with some power and with some authority and with some dignity. You must accept his authority that the situation was so grave, otherwise he would not have done so. The prime minister gave the assurance that he would hold himself personally

47

responsible for any abuse of power, and that he would give an account to the people of his stewardship at the right time. I believe that his speech may become a classic. I have never known it put so correctly, so exactly, with so much dignity, and with so much democratic certainty. In the quote from his speech, the prime minister declared his own distaste at invoking emergency powers.

"I assure you," he said, "that the government recognizes its grave responsibility at interfering in certain cases with civil liberties, and that it remains answerable to the people of Canada for its action." He was worried and he talked about the nature of the FLQ crisis. He talked about the way the FLQ was set up, its parallel of power with the presumption of being a party and a political action. He denounced it on those grounds. It's a coincidence that Trudeau and Grierson thought alike on that score. That knowledge comes from that famous interview where Trudeau says, "Well, just watch me. I think that society must take every means at its disposal to defend itself against the emergence of a parallel power which defies the elected power in this country, and I think that goes at any distance. So long as there is a power in here that is challenging the elected representatives of the people, I think that power ought to be stopped, and I think that it's only, I repeat, only these weak-kneed bleeding hearts who are afraid to take these measures." Grierson was worried. He thought that maybe Trudeau would be pushed too far. He had immense powers under the War Measures Act, and that in itself was a precarious situation. He felt that his natural allies in the country should be coming out. At one point, he suggested convening the privy council during the height of the crisis. Not only did he have a tremendous table of references — from Plato to Mao — the great philosophers of western and Oriental thought, as his references, but he had gained real knowledge of Canada, its political system, its rules of government, and party politics. He understood when those rules of party politics should be abandoned, when they should be used positively and creatively.

Another coincidence. I've already pointed out how he spoke like Trudeau, in the case of the FLQ crisis. I remember receiving a postcard from Scotland. I had written him a letter to ask if he was doing any writing. He replied, "Yes, I've been doing a bit of writing, and I've come to the nub of it," then he said, "as it is — how communications can help man meet tomorrow." In rereading Plato, a passage from *The Republic*, I was struck by Socrates' definition of ethics. He defines the good by bringing the good to the light of reason in its universality and this is what he says: "This may be done. It is good for me and what is good for me is useful to me, but what is useful to man?" That is similar to Grierson's statement about how, through communications, man meets tomorrow. In closing, I wonder what Grierson would say about the constitutional debate going on now. I suppose we can guess. Thank you very much.

TOM DALY

The Growth of a Craft: My Debt to Legg and Grierson

I DON'T KNOW if Grierson ever stuck to one subject. As a well-trained Griersonian, I'm sure I won't stick to one subject. Furthermore, I'm told I talk too much, so they very carefully arranged that we start late and that I should finish early so you can have a coffee break! There are many things I'd like to say and I'll try to pass on a few of them, and hope they happen to hit on something that interests you.

First of all I want to say that, though I was with the Grierson gang from very early, I was never one of his close ones. I was very envious of those people who were frequently closeted with him or taken everywhere with him. Still, it was all quite marvellous, and in due course I found my own close person there, who happened to be Stuart Legg, from whom I learned just about everything of the craft I have now that could possibly be learned from anybody else. And I'd like to say that I think Legg's body of work was one of the reasons that Grierson did so well at the Film Board. Legg is far too unsung and unknown. He was always rather shy of appearing in public. Unfortunately his health would not permit him to attend this seminar, for which I'm very sorry. But the last time I saw him he was just as giving as he always was.

Although I was not so close to Grierson, nobody ever kept you away from him. He was always in the kitchens at all the parties, and of course holding forth against all comers. Because I knew nothing, I was always a listener, not a partaker. There were all the articulate Alan Adamsons and Margaret Anns who were taking a full part in things. This was all a great eye-opener to me. But at the same time I think that I was influenced by Grierson as much as anybody in our generation, though not so much through his ideas at that time as by his *being*. It was simply an experience to have someone around us who had a sense of the wholeness of things and how everything related together, whether it concerned practical small things, or the entire world scene in which our little parts fitted somewhere. He seemed to be able to show how each one's little part related to everybody else's little part, and that they all had a common purpose and the possibility of a common work with a practical result, worth-while in the world.

This kind of influence on us was very exciting and very positive. And to have such a person actually in charge of a government department, and able to carry out, in his own sphere, actual works with this kind of aim and purpose and quality and vision, was for me quite astonishing.

I came to see him the first time not at all with any intent to get into film work. I came because two other letters of introduction failed because the two people I wanted to see were away for a week. And the third letter, which I hadn't sought, but which was given to me at the last moment, to see a man called John Grierson, was all I had left to try. This was in 1940, and I was seeking some kind of informational, counter-propaganda job somewhere. Well, he showed me in ten seconds that I knew nothing about film, that I knew nothing about Toronto, from where I came, that I knew nothing of any value to him and his work. I was entirely content to realize this and ready to go away and get out of his way, but he surprised me by saying, "Write me notes for a film on Toronto." I couldn't fit this in with everything else he had said. He pushed me out the door, saying, "I'll pay you thirty dollars for it." It took me two weeks to recover and hand in something — which was no good — but he asked me to try again. And that led to something.

The last time I saw Grierson was at one of his McGill seminars in his own apartment. He had called me up right in the middle of things and just said, "I want you to come down this afternoon and talk to my students about editing." And, well, you can always arrange something for Grierson. So I found myself in his apartment with about thirty people whom he was entertaining in a very informal way — this was about three or four months before he died — and I had the totally unlikely experience of being put up in front of his people and asked to hold forth in front of him. He sat at the back and didn't take part except once, when somebody asked a question, and he said, "No questions. You're here to listen, from four o'clock to six o'clock. After six you can ask all the questions you like on your own time. You're here to listen!" And he wouldn't even help me by challenging me. I was just stuck, as I feel a bit stuck today in front of all of you, with the same inner question: "What do I really know?"

Well, somehow I realized that if he did not challenge me on that occasion, and if he had invited me to speak, then somehow, somewhere, I had acquired some of the kind of life education that, it seems to me, was his aim among all of us. He didn't want imitation. He didn't want personal cults. But there was something he did want, and I just had the feeling that I'd come home. He was very quiet, and I felt in a certain sort of way that this was a point at which other people had to take over and do something on their own.

I want now to try to suggest what actually happened to me between that first visit and the last visit. Obviously, *something* had happened that really made a difference to me and to my work. And because I think it's more central than anything else, I would like to give you a few glimpses into the moments in my own life when something — something important to me — happened. In an odd way I now know they had something to do with my craft. But at the time I was unaware of it.

The first little inkling I can remember was not actually with Grierson but before, in university, when I had to read *Bleak House*, Dickens' novel. As I was reading it, I wasn't enjoying it. I just couldn't get interested in it, and we were about to be examined on it. I got into one of those personal binds where I *had* to find my interest in it in order to do anything with it, and I *couldn't*. And it seems to me this is a perfect life situation. So in desperation I thought to myself, "The next things that I can really care about in this book I'm going to write down." And at the end of the book, I had nineteen single sentences, which were all that I actually cared about in *Bleak House*. I hadn't even looked at them till the end. I just kept adding, and it all amounted to about a page and a half of foolscap. When finally I looked at them, I was absolutely startled, because about seventeen of them had the same characteristic. And I can still remember three of them exactly.

One was about a horse, in the winter, with a sleigh. It had a bell harness on. And he described how "The horse shook his head and sprinkled out a little shower of bell-ringing" and I thought, "Something wonderful about that!" The next one was about somebody's voice: "He spoke in a muffled, half-buttoned-up voice." And the third one was also about a voice: "She spoke in a cold, harsh, imperious voice which impressed my fancy as if it had a sort of spectacles on too."

And I began to realize, as I looked at all these examples, that there was, in each one, a picture image and a sound image that literally had nothing to do with each other, and yet they gave identical impressions. But that wasn't the wonder. The wonder was that the writer and I had a "something" somewhere in us that could be aware of that identity, aware of what they had in common, and, in fact, not only perceive it but, perhaps, come upon or invent new examples. And this brought me back to something that we were actually taught in my college career: the old idea of the "common sensorium" — *commune sensorium* — the place where all your senses meet, and where they can all be evaluated relative to one another, to see if they are in harmony or disharmony, or whatever. It's the origin of the term "common sense" — that's where the phrase comes from.

Now that was for me a special moment. I went to the professor and said, "Look, I'm not interested in anything else. Can I write about that?" And he said, "Please do! Everything else I've had from the students has been a rehash of something in the library. But," he said, "I've never heard of this." So I thought, "Well, I'm onto something real about education."

You can see how that developed later into a question of craft, of relating sound to picture in film in every sort of way. I don't need to go into the details. We spoke of music yesterday. We haven't really gone into sound effects yet. But they're all part of the same thing.

Okay, then, finally I got to the Film Board. The first revelation in the Board was during the time when Grierson had not yet got political control of the Motion Picture Bureau. At that time, he and Frank Badgley, who was mentioned elsewhere, had both to sign memos — because one was the Film Board, the other was the Motion Picture Bureau. They had signed that I should go down and work at the Bureau, but when Grierson wanted me back Badgley wouldn't sign, so I was stuck there — I didn't know this — and Hawes — Stanley Hawes — was in charge of trying to give me something to do at the Bureau. He gave me a clean-up job. There was a room almost as big as this room, full of cans of nitrate film, open, shut, on reels, off reels, outs, trims, dupes, sound prints, negative sound rolls — all sorts of things, and all of it very dangerous — which I also really didn't know. And they asked me to clean all this up, keep what was useful, and catalogue it, because it might be useful to other people making films. I couldn't be more grateful to Stanley Hawes — I'm sorry he's not here today to hear it — for giving me this job.

First of all I had to start asking everybody "What is this?" "What was that?" "Who did that?" and get to meet all the people. Jim Beveridge, over there, was my main mentor at the time. He told me where to go to find everybody. So I met them all, and I catalogued these things, and for the first time became absolutely necessary and useful at the Film Board, because if anybody wanted a stock shot they had to come to me.

Now, that did something for me, though again I didn't realize it at the time. Since people were asking for something that would suit this purpose or that purpose I began to look at an image not for its original purpose but for all the other possible purposes it had in it. I began to see that every image has many possible meanings depending on the centre of attention and the framing and so on, but it is still limited. There are certain ranges of meaning that it can have, lots that it cannot have, and it would be phony to try to force those meanings out of it. But I got used to thinking about all the possible meanings of a shot, without realizing that I was doing it. So you can see, again, how this is going to relate to craft later on. I should say that my real craft is film editing. Although most of my life I've been mainly a producer, I still edit occasionally, and right now, happily, I am editing one of Colin Low's films. And I'm enjoying it even more than producing.

But the steps whereby all this was developing continue: Stuart Legg was having to make films about the "World in Action," subjects he could not go and shoot all over the world, so he had to get a lot of material from the newsreels. Because I had this stock-shot capability, I was perhaps most useful to him, as compared with any other work I might have been assigned to at the Board. I was not an original location director or anything of that kind, but I was already very interested in and excited about this other kind of possibility, and I became Legg's general assistant. In the Griersonian manner, Legg was well-trained in everything. He could perform any film-making function, but he was an absolutely great editor. He was also an excellent writer, and a clear thinker. I suggest that the qualities and standards of the work that he did, which were refined down to the telling word of commentary and the exact frame of picture, set the level of standards for the rest of us to reach for in the years to come. In the cutting room, Legg explained to me aloud, as if he was thinking to himself, everything that he was doing. You know, like "This shot is moving from left to right, I'll put it up there; and this one's going from right to left, I'll keep that separate." And I began to hear him thinking aloud all the various things that were in the shots, not just the image meaning but the movement and what that did to something else. And when he was assembling a film, I began to guess what shot he would call for next and pick it off the bin before he asked for it. Then, if that *was* the one he wanted, I knew I was right, and could see that I was following his thinking. But if he asked for another one, the fact that I had to put this one back and take another meant that there was something I was missing. So I would ask him why. And he would answer. And that way I got to know much, much more about the inner workings of a person who was in fact a great teacher. Unfortunately very few people had access to him. He was just too busy. In fact, everyone was too busy.

Very many things he told me, but one of them turned out to be generically more important than any other. And this was that, in film editing, the attention moves about in the frame, following whatever is happening. And wherever the attention is at the cut, that's the point on the screen where the action of the next shot must begin, if you want continuity. And even the direction of movement must follow. The attention should continue as smoothly as if there had been no cut.

This discovery went with something else I had learned at university, in my Greek class on the *Iliad*, which was taught by my other favourite teacher, E.T. Owen: he had said that the emotional line of the *Iliad*, or any other work, was not the line of the emotions in the *Iliad*. Somebody could be laughing in the story, but you could be crying. It was the line of the emotions *you* went through following it.

Legg said practically the same thing, that the film is the line of attention you go through, and if you break that line, the connection is gone. I began to really think about that, and watch how it worked. In fact, I find this does something to your view of life. I now have come to the conclusion that attention and the study of attention is very important to our life itself. Did you ever stop to think that you cannot know anything, remember anything, or even be aware of experiencing anything, unless your attention has fallen on it at the time?

There are thousands of different things in this room, but you can only have any awareness of those that your attention has touched.

Everything else is unknown to you. It's the same with what's missing. If your attention has not noticed its absence, you don't even know it's not there to "not know." It's simply a blank, but you are unaware of it being a blank. You don't have any connection with it. Our entire conscious life is, in fact, this thin little measly line of what our attention has fallen on, and most of that is attracted away from us, without our will almost, by everything unintentional, just frittered away with commercials and God knows what. Everybody else wants to take it from us, but it is the priceless matter with which to connect with our own life.

So you see I am now very aware that the craft is not something we're just going to do cleverly, as if we're going to do this marvellous film and everybody's going to be so pleased about it. We can only put into the craft what we have already understood. I might add, particularly in a craft dealing with actuality, there's a special advantage there. In the case of a craft based on the imaginary, you build an imaginary world and get to know something about it, but what you learn may not fit real life. But in the case of a craft based on the actual, whatever you learn from it has to fit real life. It's one of those fortunate chances that I had. I now realize that the craft itself becomes your teacher, your own teacher, and thereby also a source of help to anyone else, at the point where either your other teachers disappear — the ones that you had and respected — or where you can't get more from them because it has to become your own understanding.

The other day I heard here that phrase, from Grierson's unknown and unpublished work, that one should "honour one's craft" and that there should be the feeling of taking a Hippocratic oath about that so that it was not just for your own personal interest but to be put in the service of something. When I heard that the other day, I thought, "That's exactly what I really do feel about our craft, whatever it may be." It can be camera, sound, anything. And of course it is the same for creative crafts other than film.

But there's still something possibly missing there. We may be deeply interested and involved, and still very narrow. We are all excited about what we want to do. We're all annoyed when the things in the world don't fit that and make it easily possible. But what to do about that? Everybody would like to change the world to fit "me" and make things comfortable and easy for "me." Most people are like that, I think. They have at least that side. Here comes the difficult part. I can exemplify it in my own case, because there was a time when I thought my craft was pretty good, and I had a very effective unit, and we were doing some very good films. It was exactly then that five of these "best friends," as I thought then, came to my apartment and said, "Look, we don't want to work with anyone else but you. But if you stay the way you are, we can't go on this way any longer." Now that, I submit, is a very key moment in one's life. There was absolutely no doubt that they were my friends; in fact, that's why they were coming to me instead of talking to other people. There was absolutely no doubt in my mind that there was something behind what they said. But I couldn't understand it. There was something missing in me, and I couldn't really catch what it was. I asked them to try to point it out when it was happening and they said, "Well, it's difficult, but we'll try." Gradually, bit by bit, this was done. To make a long long story short, I want to bring you to what I concluded from all this after many years. My conclusion is that most of us, if not all of us, are lopsided people. We think we are all-round, because we have a taste of everything — thoughts, feelings, actions, sensations, and so on — and we exchange talk about it all with other people. But it seems to me that just about everybody still tends to be lopsided, either in the intellectual way (the intellectual person), or the emotional way (the emotional person), or the physical way (the physical person). Although everybody has this feeling of being *all* of that, in fact one of these elements dominates nearly everybody. So that, for instance, the intellectual person thinks how life should be, sets a plan: "Nine o'clock to five o'clock is the right time to work," or whatever — "This is right, I've decided it." He tries to live by that — but it never works. The feelings don't fit, and things don't work out that way. They are always justified in theory. But it isn't enough.

Or the emotional person: His "great marvellous work" goes on — when he feels like it. When he doesn't feel like it, he can't work at all, or it's awful work. He can't think, because, for him, what is right is what he likes, and everything he doesn't like is wrong, and so on.

The physical person can work very well. "If you're going to walk a tight-rope, don't think about it, keep your feelings out of it, and you'll be fine." But when the work actually needs independent thought or feeling it can't be done.

You start to trust that one thing that you like best, and you leave the other things unformed because you're not very good at them, not very comfortable with them, and they atrophy or don't develop. This one thing dominates everything.

For instance, in the case of self-pity, the self-pity begins to select, in people's minds, only the thoughts that magnify this self-pity. They talk to everybody about it. They complain about everything. They keep it going. They try to get the help and attention of other people to increase the self-pity. Their attitude, their physical posture, the tone of their voice, all goes with that, and they do everything, not to solve it, but to keep it going.

Well, I leave you to work some of this out by yourself. But I began to see, as a film producer, how a director may be one type of person, the cameraman another type. They're not understanding each other. At least two "head" people can agree on the terms of reference they are disagreeing about. But how do you evaluate the feeling person and the intellectual person together when they are lopsided? How do they meet? Back to *Bleak House* and the *common sensorium*. There is a place in everybody where you can relate the qualities and values, the harmoniousness or disharmoniousness, or whatever, of different things — and, also, of different people. It's true, there's nothing wrong with a completely emotional poem, or a completely intellectual dissertation, or a completely physical sculpture — that's all good. But it could be greater, within the same film length, if it had all those elements together.

What about all this when you are confronted with making a film? It's more than a question of just getting a team together. If they are all of one kind, they are totally limited by their common lacks. If they are of different kinds, how do you relate them? It's not just them: the producer is also lopsided. The program people are lopsided. The sponsor is lopsided: if you talk in your own language and he understands another one, how are you going to get the money? It really begins to be important for your craft to grow beyond a certain point of limitation.

Take the 1960s, for instance. You had a very wonderful thing happening from one point of view. People no longer wanted to imitate. I thought that was great, because they really wanted, as they said, to "be themselves" — one very important element. But the other side of it was that they thought that, *as they were*, they were already great and developed. This was the part I didn't and don't agree with. Practically nobody is that great just because they are "doing what they like" now.

I really began to understand Grierson's ideas, the very things that I wasn't able to appreciate when I first came. They are starting to express for me in words the experiences I was actually having. In a funny kind of way I'm coming around to those at the last, where many others of my friends started with that and went on to other things. I think this is what is so wonderful about Grierson's total view. Since everything fitted together in a totality, it didn't matter where you started in that totality, it led to as much of all the rest as you could reach. It didn't matter whether it was with him and in his lifetime or whether it continued afterward. In fact, for me, one of the great things is that it does continue once the process gets started, and you have the feeling about it that your craft is a craft to honour.

I could go into all kinds of details about editing. There are lots of things I'd love to say. But I think it's still more important for anybody to reach such a feeling about their own work that they are unsatisfied unless, on the one hand, it is the best they can do at that moment, and, on the other hand, that it is also speaking to someone else, in terms that the other can understand. In other words, it is important to exercise and develop the little "something" that is maybe the *common sensorium*. I now would dare to call it one's conscience. This is where you can feel everything simultaneously without being afraid of the contradictions that you have, but in a kind of objective way, which is exactly similar to the way you feel things about others. It does happen sometimes that you touch this, and, when you do, I find that it is the source both of relationship to yourself and of relationship to others. It's one and the same thing! So there's only one thing to learn, so to speak.

If I may just take five minutes more, I would like to tell about a personal experience that was another key moment in my life. It was connected with anger, behind which I discovered fear. I couldn't get past the fears. The details are not important, but the fears were about all kinds of big things. I had the feeling that, if I tried to tackle them head-on, I would die, I would be snuffed out. I couldn't get past that. At the same time I had some friends who said, "There's much more to you than you think. Just go ahead and tackle it, and you'll find out." It sounded great.

But they had other characteristics, and I thought to myself, "They don't know what it's like to feel like I do. They're just wrong. I know this is true for myself. They can do it but I can't." I thought about it every way I could. Finally I guess I gave up trying

59

to force a resolution. About two weeks later I was just sitting on my bed, blankly, when I had the most amazing flash of understanding. It all came in a moment, but I have to explain it in order. It was something like this: there was in front of me a constant fire, which represented what I was afraid of. The inconsistencies in me were represented by the fact that at one moment I was like oxygen, and if I tried to approach the fire I would just feed it and be snuffed out. I really would die. At another time I was like hydrogen, and that was even worse because in approaching the fire I would also feed it, but this time I would go up — "Bang!" Everybody would look and see what a discomfiture I had. That was horrifying. So the image showed me, you see, that I was right: I could try for ever and ever to force this fear away, and I couldn't do it.

But the image also said, "Look, hydrogen and oxygen combine to make water. Water is not afraid of fire. Your friends are right. There is more to it than that. It can be done — not by continuing the old way of forcing, but by finding the means to integration," another Grierson word, as I've heard this week. Whatever that bond is, whatever that force is, that can connect all these disconnected parts and relate them together, if that can be sought and if it really lives in us, then, oddly enough, all those parts that are impossible separately, together, like atoms in a chemical mixture, can form into one total, like a new molecule, which has different characteristics and a totally other response to the world. Most of the things you would have been trying to change in the world, like getting rid of fire, cease to be problems. Water can put out fire. The problem is gone.

So I want to suggest that there really is something about craft which, if you take it as your teacher, begins to give you something back, and begins to open up this "something-in-common," which not only accepts all your own parts and inconsistencies but also those of other people in the world — without exception, perhaps.

Now, why go into that at this moment? Well, when you have an impact on you, there seem to be three ways it can go. One of them is when you are afraid, and there's suppression. That way is poison and death. The second is when you kick away this extra pressure. If you were insulted, you insult back. If you were hit, you hit back. That way leads to violence. I think it's the source of violence in the world. It solves no problems and only serves to continue or escalate them. The third way, which is something that I didn't understand for a long time, is to use that pressure as the force to produce the molecule from the parts, the thing that holds the whole thing together, and that way lies understanding. It has a different functioning in oneself and in the world.

All through this conference, the things people have been quoting from Grierson and his books and his speeches all point in the same direction for me. I'm just beginning to understand that his words were always telling us such things, in his way, and I'm trying to affirm — through what I got from him, and from Legg, and from Hawes, and from all my friends — that it's the same world we're talking about. That's the hope, because there really is something that we can do in order to relate to others. Films really can make a difference to others.

I've been very impressed by the group content here, but I am sad that there isn't a contingent of two hundred young people arguing and pushing and twisting and turning to dump the rest of us and do something, of the same quality all right, but something now and something for the future. I think there are too many of us old people here, happily talking to each other, and not enough of those who will be responsible for the future. It is especially a pity because I think that the bunch of young film-makers that have been turning up and working around us in the last few years is the nearest thing to the group of people that I remember Grierson collecting around him. For a long time there was a kind of cult of "my film," you know, special titles indicating "A film by So-and-So." But I am finding, and perhaps it's because of what's happening in the world, that there are far more young film-makers now who are caring about their work, the standard of work, their craft, including the ideas in it and the images in it and the honesty of feeling in it. They also work in teams. They care about the community and their audiences. They try to serve them with something meaningful. I, for one, am very hopeful of the body of work they will accomplish, and am glad to entrust to their care the continuation of the Griersonian tradition.

JACK ELLIS

John Grierson's Relation with British Documentary During World War Two

GRIERSON was in Canada from just before the outbreak of war, in 1939, until shortly after its cessation, in 1945. Though enormously busy during those years, as head of the National Film Board and, more briefly, the Wartime Information Board, he maintained his contacts with the British documentary movement, which he had founded and led during the decade preceding the war.

The relationship between Grierson and his former colleagues makes me think of the father who has left home. Though he hovered over his "children" with affection, he seemed to feel increasing puzzlement and some dismay at the directions they were taking (or not taking). They, for their part, at first, perhaps, felt his absence keenly and did seem uncertain in their movements. Then they gained new strength and assurance, reaching a peak of accomplishment during wartime. But those same years saw the remarkable coherence that had existed in the British documentary group begin to diminish. Grierson never completely regained his leadership in the post-war years.

Writing in 1941 to Arthur Elton, one of his former colleagues, about the changes required of British documentary by the war, Grierson looked back at their efforts in the thirties. "It was fine in that brave decade of ours," he wrote. "We were a liberal force wearing away the props of complacency. We hadn't a chance of winning, or winning in time, without a political movement to use us; and that failed, for us, when the Labour movement lost its internal steam after the general strike [of 1926]."[1] On the other hand, he thought that "Without *Housing Problems* and the whole movement of social understanding such films helped to articulate... history would have found another bloodier solution when the bombs first rained on the cities of Britain."[2] Cryptic though this statement is, by "bloodier solution" he may have meant revolution and defeat.

One might not regard the British documentaries of the 1930s as preparing a country to accept and persist in a war. In fact, one might be inclined to fault the Griersonian system of "general consent" as not allowing for the sort of anti-fascist films the Americans somehow managed to produce, in the 1930s, outside governmental and industrial sponsorship. Yet, though not dealing directly with politics or war, the British documentaries quietly and steadily pushed attitudes that would be most helpful: getting the job done, social co-operation, the obligation to be informed, the value of government service. Perhaps Grierson was right, to one degree or another.

However, despite (maybe in part because of) his hovering attention over the movement he had founded, there developed during the war the first evident strain in the loyalties of the British group towards Grierson — some fierce arguments and some defections. Part of this was brought on by his steady criticism of the propaganda approach of the British documentaries, and, in fact, of Britain's wartime stance, offered in private and public correspondence. In a letter from Australia to Elton in March of 1940, Grierson conceded that the war may have been doing some good in making the English think about what other people thought of them. At the same time he felt that England insisted on seeing every event in political — national — terms and missed the "boundary-crossings in economic terms of world events." He complained that England looked forward to a post-war world in which things would be back to normal rather than seeing the "need for new economic integration."[3]

II

During the war, Grierson returned briefly to Britain at least twice. Michael Spencer, one of the National Film Board young men, remembered him as a passenger on a troop ship in August of 1941.[4] Perhaps it was this visit that Edgar Anstey, English documentary veteran, told a story about.

Anstey had been trying to get Grierson, who was staying with him, to go see the people of London bedding down in the tube in

63

preparation for the night's raids by the Luftwaffe. Grierson resisted, on the grounds that Anstey's interest and pride in their ability to endure was merely another evidence of the British defensive position (as in *London Can Take It*), whereas Grierson favoured a more positive, aggressive approach. He said, according to Anstey, "Oh, you people sentimentalize all that. I know about it from reading about it." When Anstey finally did succeed in getting him down into the tube shelters, he was tremendously impressed and moved — like Henry Moore of the marvellous series of shelter sketches. In a characteristic about-face, Grierson talked about it for a week to everybody he saw and demanded to know why the British film-makers weren't putting that great story on the screen.[5] By October 8, he was in Lisbon on his way back to Canada.[6] Basil Wright, another of Grierson's former lieutenants, surmised that he had visited England mainly to talk with Jack Beddington, head of the Films Division of the Ministry of Information, regarding Canadian films in Britain and British films in Canada.[7]

Much better documented is a trip in 1944. Grierson arrived in London in mid-July and returned to Ottawa in mid-August.[8] During that stay, not long after D-Day, he also visited France. In a talk over CBC radio, on August 20, he noted that "Two Sundays ago at this hour I was driving in a jeep from Brittany to a Canadian encampment near Caen. This was the day before the great Canadian breakthrough from Caen toward Falaise." His own special mission, he said, was "to see and talk to the film and still photographers who were up there in the front line, sending back the pictures of action." Incidentally, that broadcast was a superb bit of war correspondence, in the Ernie Pyle manner, only better, with vivid details of the French countryside, of soldiers, and operations.[9]

III

In the September 1940 *Documentary News Letter* there appeared a communique from "a correspondent in America" dated August 10. On the basis of internal stylistic evidence, the "correspondent" seems to me pretty clearly to have been Grierson, anonymous possibly so as not to offend former colleagues or to put his personal weight behind this criticism, mild and positive as it was. Or, as it would turn out, anonymous perhaps so as not to become the target of counter-attacks. In any case, it was the first instance of the

64

former leader publicly rapping the knuckles of the former fellow workers, and just preceded the affair of the speech at the end of *Foreign Correspondent,* which would increase the friction and will be dealt with presently.

The American correspondent was critical of British documentary and semi-documentary production reaching Canada and the United States as being "too little and too late." He felt it was the job of the British documentarians to make the "American spirit feel at one with the English spirit," and complained about the "inept resuscitation of the snob message" in the film *King's People,* which was about Canada. "Ironically," he offered, "the people who are trying hardest — and perhaps do best — are not the English but the Americans. Walter Wanger's *Foreign Correspondent* and *Long Voyage Home* are typical of that effort."[10] Another "American Correspondent," in the following issue, gently and partially disengaged himself or herself from Grierson (it seems to me likely that the writer was Mary Losey, a prime mover in efforts to organize documentary in the United States) before going on to attack *Foreign Correspondent.* "With the general criticism in the article I am in entire agreement; but there are some statements of fact which make it obvious that the writer knows intimately about films in Canada and not so completely about films in the United States."[11] The major battle, however, would be fought along the lines of Grierson's implications that the British didn't know or weren't doing their job, and the British reply that Grierson did not understand their situation and was not qualified to talk from another country that wasn't experiencing the war in the manner they were — in short, that his criticism and advice were ill-informed and possibly in bad taste.

In the January 1941 letter to Elton already mentioned, Grierson had much to say about the parochial, selfish, class-ridden view of England, which still expected the world to look to her and had lost the real picture of the world — that it was increasingly a small country prepared to go down with its own bravery, savoring courage in defeat, as it were. In the same letter, he also argued at length that rather than completed documentaries, British footage should be sent over to be made into films for Americans by people, for example himself and Stuart Legg, an Englishman producing at the Film Board, who knew the mentality.[12] In general he thought reportage better for American audiences than documentary: that the Americans thought fast and in a straight line; that the English were slower but more complex and devious.[13] Admitting the quality of *London Can Take It*, he wanted instead films of people "doing something about the war, doing something, not feeling something sadly and wearily à la Quentin Reynolds," the American war correspondent who wrote and read the commentary for *London Can Take It.*[14]

Writing to Basil Wright in October of 1941, Grierson expressed the view that the British film-makers didn't have as much freedom within the government as the Canadians did — that they had to make only what the government wanted. He also repeated the theme that England was not looking to the future (or present), and re-emphasized the geopolitical advantages of Canada and the global concerns in an air age. The British view was too parochial, he again charged, rooted in tradition: it was a tight little island. Some of this complaint seemed to stem from his acknowledgement that Beddington, of the MOI, had felt that the Canadian films were too removed from — ahead of — the British position and were not suitable for showing in the United Kingdom.[15] Grierson was trying to instill his "old boys" with his own viewpoint and get them to push it. Wright observed that the documentary people had earlier wanted Grierson to return to the United Kingdom as Minister of Information, but that there had been no offers from the government.[16]

Regarding Grierson's views of Canadian merits and British shortcomings, Anstey amusedly recalled that on the 1944 visit Grierson had some young Canadian film-makers with him, whom he put in an awkward position by praising them and pointing out the old fuddy-duddies of British documentary.[17] After that visit, however, he wrote for *Documentary News Letter* in a conciliatory, if somewhat contradictory, vein: "It has been a wonderful thing to see, in spite of the war and the special difficulties of film-making in Britain, the documentary people there have remembered the essentials of social reference. They have not been fooled into the fallacy that fighting films give anything more than one layer of the present reality." Still, he had a "but", which foreshadowed some of the difficulty documentary would encounter in post-war Britain: "I keep on feeling that the documentary group as a whole is not at the centre where political and social planning is being thought out and legislated, or not close enough to the centre. It is not good enough to be on the outside looking in, waiting on someone else's pleasure for an opportunity to serve social progress."[18]

66

IV

There was also the brouhaha over *Foreign Correspondent*, the 1940 release produced by Walter Wanger and directed by Alfred Hitchcock. Grierson, as "a correspondent in America," had praised the film. Mary Losey, if she was the "American Correspondent," disagreed with him and took strong exception to the film: "Not only to me, but to many others who have complained bitterly, it is incredible that Wanger and Hitchcock would have devised a noble and heroic death for their fifth-column politician, followed by a justification of his way of life from his daughter. Is this what we are to expect when 'Hollywood tries hard'?"

But the furor in Britain centred around another scene. At the end of the film Joel Macrea, a correspondent modelled on Quentin Reynolds and/or Edward R. Murrow, broadcasts to America from a London radio studio. The crucial monologue is as follows:

> I can't read the rest of the speech I had because all the lights have gone out — so I'll have just to talk off the cuff. All that noise you hear isn't static. It's death coming to London. Yes, they're coming here now. You can hear the bombs falling on the streets and the homes. Don't tune me out. Hang on a while. This is a big story — and you're a part of it. It's too late to do anything here now except stand in the dark and let them come. It's as if the lights are out everywhere — except in America. Keep those lights burning there. Cover them with steel; ring them with guns. Build a canopy of battleships and bombing planes around them — Hello, America! Hang onto your lights. They're the only lights left in the world![19]

Although it reviewed *Foreign Correspondent* quite favorably as the "Film of the Month," *Documentary News Letter* nevertheless felt it necessary to address itself quite specifically to the Macrea speech. "The importance of the sequence is that it is a message to the States — and not to us — sent out by an American journalist and, in fact, conceived at script conferences at which Walter Wanger had the last word." The latter part of this statement was a veiled allusion to a rumour starting to circulate that it was Grierson who had written the final speech for his friend Wanger. *DNL* went on: "It is neither a warlike nor a political piece of propaganda; it stimulates thought, and its message should strike home on the other side of the Atlantic; to us over here it does at least bring evidence of a good will backed by clear thinking."[20]

The *DNL* reviewer's opinion was not, however, held unanimously among the British documentary people, and Paul Rotha started a public debate with a letter published in the succeeding issue. Of the speech, Rotha said, "I describe it as an insult to the 'only army which,' claims *DNL* itself in an editorial in the same issue, 'will win the war'; an army of civilians, I maintain, in whom the lights have never burned more brightly and more proudly than they do now." Further, "I can assure these leaders of the British documentary film that the people who are really suffering as well as fighting this war do not share this view that the lights are even dimmed in Britain. If they did, the Fascist propagandists might well claim to have already won the war."[21]

As for Grierson's part in the indignity, Rotha wrote:

> The tale has gone the rounds that the words spoken by Macrea were either written or inspired by Mr. John Grierson when he was in Hollywood. If this is true (though to me they sound more like Mr. Kennedy [presumably Joseph Kennedy, United States Amabassador to the Court of St. James] than Mr. Grierson) they reveal a grave lack of knowledge of public opinion in Britain, a lack one does not usually associate with a propagandist so sensitive to the public pulse as Mr. Grierson.
>
> My own belief is that if the Editors of *DNL* had not been under the impression that the words in question had been written or inspired by Mr. John Grierson, they might not have been so quick to agree that their own, as well as other people's beliefs in democratic Britain had vanished. Assuming he is responsible, Mr. Grierson's 4,000 odd miles remove from Britain may explain his rare misjudgment of public opinion, but Film Centre Ltd. [which published *Documentary News Letter*] is, after all, quite close to the Front Line.

Others who wished "to associate their names with this letter" were Michael Balcon, Ealing Studios; Ritchie Calder, *Daily Herald* and *New Statesman*; Alberto Cavalcanti, Ealing Studios; A.J. Cummings, *News Chronicle*; Aubrey Flanagan, *Motion Picture*

Herald; Michael Foot, *Evening Standard*; Dilys Powell, *Sunday Times*; and Grierson's old friend from Glasgow University days, Alexander Werth, *Manchester Guardian*.[22] It is interesting that Cavalcanti was the only documentary film-maker among this group.

In the next issue of *Documentary News Letter* Brian Smith wrote:

> The speech at the end of *Foreign Correspondent* has aroused such distinguished controversy that someone should record the simple probability: it has not the same meaning on the screen as in print.
>
> Maybe James Hilton, Charles Bennett, Joan Harrison, John Grierson and other stray advisers from Hollywood's British colony failed to see the tactlessness of the words, but I guess Hitch directed for the effect, and it's the screen effect which matters: argument ignoring this is academic.[23]

With this, the allegations and arguments were allowed to drop from view.

Publicly Grierson remained silent but in a letter to Basil Wright in December of 1940 he said that he did not write the *Foreign Correspondent* speech and that it did not represent his view. If he didn't quite echo Rotha's assertion that the lights weren't even dimmed in Britain, he did feel that they were just beginning to come up. In terms of North America and relating it to Europe he approved the ending and deplored Rotha's having written his letter.

V

Even before the *Foreign Correspondent* controversy, another divisive argument had started that would last longer and prove much more basic and damaging. It revolved around the relative contributions and different views of Grierson (propaganda) and Cavalcanti (aesthetics) in British documentary, and would finally centre on a feature-length anthology made up of excerpts from famous documentaries compiled by Cavalcanti and by Ernest Lindgren who belonged to the British Film Institute. Its title was *Film and Reality*.

The rivalry started, publicly at least, in a curious, indirect manner. In the April-May, 1940 issue of *Cine-Technician*, published by the Association of Cine-Technicians (ACT), Kenneth Gordon, who regularly wrote the column "Cinema Log," told a story about Cavalcanti's being hauled off to a police station because of his foreign accent while shooting *Squadron 992* in Scotland. Gordon concluded: "I dare say that the local cops are still rather puzzled as to why British film technicians should have foreign accents."

Basil Wright, in a letter in the June-July issue, reproached Gordon for his ungrateful chauvinism and testified to Cavalcanti's great contribution to British documentary. Gordon, replying to Wright in the same issue, wrote that wages and conditions at Cavalcanti's unit (the General Post Office Film Unit, which would soon become the Crown Film Unit) were bad and that the ACT had experienced difficulties in negotiating with him. Also, somewhat gratuitously, Gordon added: "I would say that the documentary movement owes more to John Grierson than anyone else" — which put Wright's good will and fairness towards Cavalcanti in a strange light of contest.

In the August-September issue, R. McNaughton, who had come to the GPO in 1934 and worked as editor and director, jumped into the fray "on behalf of some of the older members." "Any technician worth his salt will admit that the genius and guidance of Cavalcanti is behind by far the majority of worthwile British documentary films." He went on to say that Cavalcanti was not responsible for the bad conditions at the GPO unit, that he had made valuable efforts on behalf of the unit, that he had displayed generosity, and so forth. "Finally," McNaughton wrote," we consider that the influence of Cavalcanti is at least equal to that of John Grierson. British documentaries have obtained a high following both at home and overseas and Cavalcanti has undoubtedly been largely responsible for this."[24]

During this time Cavalcanti and Lindgren had begun production of *Film and Reality*, with its survey of the international development of documentary up to 1940. When it was released early in 1942 it was reviewed by Basil Wright in the March issue of *Documentary News Letter*. Wright identified and, to an extent, rekindled the running controversy when he wrote that the film was, to himself at least, "in many places controversial as regards its choice of material, and its attitude towards the social, as opposed to the academic or aesthetic development of the realist film."[25] What

Cavalcanti had done (the selection and interpretation of the examples were his) was to treat documentary as an evolving artistic discipline, the impetus for which had been to render the raw fact of the material world into aesthetic form ("the creative treatment of actuality," after all, Grierson had first written). Cavalcanti's selections comprised the most dramatic and loveliest sequences from a large number of films going back to pre-documentary origins. No mention was made of the educational-social preoccupations of the British (or for that matter the Soviet) school. Significantly, following the title "The Realistic Documentary of Life at Home," British documentary was lumped with various continental efforts, including the City Symphony films and highly stylized sports films. The final section was devoted to "Realism in the Story Film." Clearly, *Film and Reality* represented a dereliction to Griersonian eyes.

Lindgren it was, rather than Cavalcanti, who responded in the following issue of *DNL* to Wright's criticisms. In his defense, Lindgren quoted from a letter by veteran documentary director Harry Watt to the *New Statesman*. "It was Grierson's drive and initiative that obtained the formation of the Empire Marketing Board Film Unit . . . it was the introduction of Cavalcanti's professional skill and incredible film sense that raised the standard and reputation of British documentary," Watt had written.

A letter from Wright was printed alongside the one from Lindgren:

> Grierson, like all great men, is well able to ignore attacks made on him from whatever motives. But in the interests of accuracy, and also because I am sure that I am expressing the feeling of documentary workers as a whole, I must point out that Grierson has always been and still is a remarkable technician, a magnificent teacher, and, in short, a great producer.

> Grierson is not merely the founder of the documentary movement. Since its inception it has been his own understanding of film technique, his encouragement of experimentation and (to meet Lindgren on his own ground) his uncanny grasp and knowledge of aesthetics as regards art in general and film art in particular, which have been the driving force and inspiration of the progress of documentary.

71

These qualities, out of deference to Lindgren, I have put first, but I must now add Grierson's political grasp and foresight, his incredible energy and organizational drive, and, above all, his unswerving loyalty not merely to the idea of documentary but to all those working for him.[26]

Wright's response is quite unprecedented in the polemics that accompanied documentary from its birth. There is no earlier public instance of this degree of personal praise of Grierson from a member of his group; any hint of a "cult of personality" was studiously avoided in Grierson's own writings and those of his associates. Lindgren did not "attack" Grierson, as Wright alleged; the closest he came to it was the quote from Watt, whose contribution to the "disloyalty" is pointedly unacknowledged by Wright. It would seem that only in the face of growing defection — Cavalcanti and Watt were the targets; Lindgren in a sense had merely stepped into the fight — could Wright be goaded into such a furious defense.

Wright's position was supported by an editorial in that same issue of *DNL*: "The documentary film movement as it was created and developed under John Grierson was and still is directed to one purpose and to one purpose only — the formation of a body of skilled propagandists trained to express their propaganda ideas by means of film."[27]

The earlier mentioned letter from Grierson, which had grown into an article, stemmed from this same controversy and was published in June of 1942. Prefaced with an explanation that it was a letter "to a member of the Editorial Board of *DNL*," readers were advised that "Its content is so important that it can be regarded as a considered and categorical article on propaganda policy." Grierson wrote:

> In our world, it is specially necessary these days to guard against the aesthetic argument.... Documentary was from the beginning — when we first separated our public purpose theories from those of Flaherty — an anti-aesthetic movement.
> What confuses history is that we had always the good sense to use the aesthetes. We did so because we liked them and because we needed them. It was, paradoxically, with the first-rate aesthetic help of people like Flaherty and

Cavalcanti that we mastered the techniques necessary for our quite unaesthetic purposes.[28]

The article, in its entirety, is indeed a marvellous statement of Grierson's purposes.

Though Grierson never wrote directly of *Film and Reality*, he was said to have hated it.[29] Some five years later, Cavalcanti ruefully recalled the events surrounding its production. The problem of "'who' did 'what' in film history and film aesthetics is a problem both involved and perilous," he wrote. "After working two solid years on a film essay about film criticism — *Film and Reality* — I burnt my fingers so painfully that I ought to know." But, still not content to let the argument rest, he continued:

> I know, too, that the use of Cinema as a social weapon is an urgent necessity. Nevertheless the exaggerated utilitarian approach to the film medium which it entails could become a reactionary influence as dangerous as the aesthetic one. The utilitarians claim that film-making ought to be reduced to the task of collecting a series of shots and accompanying them by a rousing election speech. They forget that by doing so they are blunting the edge of their weapon.[30]

Going beyond mere arguing, some of the veterans were leaving documentary in the direction of the fiction film. The same year that *Film and Reality* was released, 1942, Cavalcanti completed his first British feature as associate producer: *The Foreman Went to France* (produced by Michael Balcon, directed by Charles Frend). Having some semi-documentary elements, the film did not represent as big a jump as one might suppose: in Britain, "the bridge between feature and documentary is shorter than anywhere else," Cavalcanti later wrote.[31] It was, after all, Harry Watt who had established the prototype for the sub-species of wartime semi-documentary with *Target for Tonight* out of Crown. The studios were merely following the documentarians' lead and Watt shortly followed Cavalcanti to Ealing to help.

If in some ways the semi-documentary represented a reaction against Grierson's first principles, it nonetheless stemmed from the movement he had founded and the people he had trained. As Grierson's editor and biographer Forsyth Hardy wrote, "It was during the war that the first unmistakable signs of documentary's impact on the studio film became apparent." If several of the documentary directors, including Cavalcanti and Watt, were making features, "the realistic approach was also adopted by other directors whose work had previously shown little tendency in that direction," Hardy continued. *One of Our Aircraft is Missing* (1942), *Next of Kin* (1942), *Millions Like Us* (1943), *San Demetrio, London* (1943), *The Way Ahead* (1944), and *Waterloo Road* (1945) "were a few of the films which applied to feature production the principles hammered out in the documentary movement."[32] At the same time, this output was being matched by the official documentary units with an increasing tendency towards feature length, narrative construction, characterization, and synchronously recorded dialogue — all standard attributes of the fiction film. The semi-documentary form, which would carry over into the post-war era, earned for documentary a much wider and more enthusiastic audience than the more austere shorts of exposition and persuasion had ever achieved. Grierson, though he may have resisted the impulse during the war years on grounds of too much aestheticism and artistic self-indulgence, would be closely associated with the semi-documentary form and even the fiction film in post-war Britain. By that time, however, the British documentary movement as movement, as Griersonian movement, at least, had ended or become diffused.

When asked whether British documentary would have come through the war in stronger array if Grierson had remained in England, Stuart Legg, the British veteran who had worked most closely with Grierson in Canada, said simply: "Possibly so, but then we would be without the Film Board."[33] I doubt that any of us would welcome such a possibility.

Legg's observation permits us to restore to their proper perspective the tensions that occurred during, and the shifts that resulted after, the war. Whatever Grierson's relationship with British documentary during World War Two, those were years of splendid accomplishment, for him in Canada and for documentary in Britain.

[1] John Grierson, letter to Arthur Elton, 28 January 1941.

[2] John Grierson, "The Documentary Idea 1942," *Documentary News Letter*, 3 (June 1942), 83-86.

[3] John Grierson, letter to Arthur Elton, 21 March 1940.

[4] Michael Spencer, interview with author, Sept. 1962.

[5] Edgar Anstey, interview with author, Aug. 1966.

[6] John Grierson, letter to Basil Wright, 8 Oct. 1941.

[7] Basil Wright, interview with author, Sept. 1966.

[8] The *Times* [London], 13 July 1944, 2e.

[9] John Grierson, "Talk on a Visit to Normandy and Brittany." CBC, 20 Aug. 1944, mimeographed, 6 pp. Published in *Documentary News Letter*, 5, No. 4 (1944), 44.

[10] "A correspondent in America," "The Other Side of the Atlantic." *Documentary News Letter*, 1 (Sept. 1944), 3-4.

[11] "American Correspondent," *Documentary News Letter*, 1 (Oct. 1944).

[12] Grierson, letter to Elton, 28 Jan. 1941.

[13] John Grierson, letter to Basil Wright, Dec. 1940.

[14] Grierson, letter to Elton, 28 Jan. 1941.

[15] Grierson, letter to Wright, 8 Oct. 1941.

[16] Wright, interview, Sept. 1966.

[17] Anstey, interview, Aug. 1966.

[18] John Grierson, "Grierson Asks for a Common Plan," *Documentary News Letter*, 5, No. 5 (1944), 49-51.

[19] As quoted by Paul Rotha, "Correspondence," *Documentary News Letter*, 1 (Dec. 1940), 19.

[20] "Film of the Month: *Foreign Correspondent*," *Documentary News Letter*, 1 (Nov. 1940), 6.

[21] Rotha, "Correspondence," *DNL* (Dec. 1940).

[22] Rotha.

[23] Brian Smith, "Correspondence: *Foreign Correspondent*," *Documentary News Letter*, 2 (Jan. 1941), 13-14.

[24] R. McNaughton, *Cine-Technician*, 6 (Aug.-Sept. 1940), 81.

[25] Basil Wright, *Documentary Film News*, 3 (March 1942), 40-42.

[26] Ernest H. Lindgren and Basil Wright, "Propaganda or Aesthetics?", *Documentary News Letter*, 3, No. 4 (April 1942), 56-58.

[27] "Notes of the Month," *Documentary News Letter*, 3, No. 4 (April 1942), 50.

[28] Grierson, "The Documentary Idea 1942."

[29] Guy Glover, interview with author, Sept. 1962.

[30] Alberto Cavalcanti, "Foreword" to Ken Cameron, *Sound and the Documentary Film* (London: Sir Isaac Pitman & Sons, 1947), pp. vii-viii.

[31] Cavalcanti, pp. vii-viii.

[32] Forsyth Hardy, "John Grierson and the Documentary Idea," *Films in 1951: A Special Publication on British Films and Film-Makers for the Festival of Britain.* (London: *Sight and Sound* for the British Film Institute, May 1951), pp. 55-56.

[33] Stuart Legg, interview with author, Sept. 1966.

MARGARET ANN ELTON

The Images of Canada:
An Appraisal of the Eye, the Mind,
and the Teaching of John Grierson

AS A GENTLE REPROACH to a gentle shade, this is not going to be a
scholarly paper, for it was Grierson who wrenched me out of the
university, abused my thesis on *The English Epic*, scorned my
attachment to the Homeric epithets in Milton, and declared that
the training of the intellect was futile unless it led to an active life
in society. Only partly persuaded that the "greatest global war in
history" was to be won by my efforts, I found fresh woods and
pastures new in the disciplined chaos of the negative cutting room,
and graduated, *cum laude* at least, in another subject that might
well be termed iconography, or the relentless pursuit of images.
Grierson may have been right. It is possible that my tutor, Thomas
Daly, and I did win the war.

Grierson is rightly associated with three Scottish universities,
Glasgow, Stirling, and McGill, and the organization of a Grierson
seminar by Professor Peter Ohlin is a poignant reminder that
McGill brought the last years of Grierson to a vigorously tranquil
end, during which, I note with barely a sigh of resentment, he was
exhorting his students to study Plato carefully. *Sic transit*. And in
Montreal, as Mary Ferguson said, "All the maples red and gold
were flaming for him." McGill was his last image of Canada.

The year in which he wrote his *Report on Canadian Government
Film Activities*, 1938, was marked, prophetically, by a mail flight
from Halifax to Seattle, and Grierson noted that a film on civil
aviation, among others, was required. He was preoccupied with an
assessment of the images of Canada as defined by the Canadian
government's Motion Picture Bureau, and his *Report* is characteristically courteous, incisive, and blunt. He deemed suitable for the
Empire Film Library at the Imperial Institute new prints of: *Where
the Moose Runs Loose, Monarch of the Rockies, The Story of a Can of
Salmon, The Story of Canadian Pine, Big Timber, Angling Across*

Canada, Fishin' the High Spots, Canada's Maple Industry, and *Beaver Family*, among others. Here we have the projection of Canada in the pre-war terms of "scenics," "tourism," and "primary products."

His list of films to be withdrawn includes a mixture, as before: *Canadian Apples, Portal of the Prairies, Where the Moose Cow Calls, The Cruise of the Sagamo, Regions of Romance,* and *Through the Norway of America.* One wonders what criteria he was invoking.

Although he retained a nostalgic regard for what he termed the "Sunset and Evening Star, and One Clear Call For Bill the Lone Fisherman" film program, his appointment as Canadian film commissioner, the outbreak of war, and his passionate commitment to a new destiny for Canada, inevitably saw the older images transformed in less than a decade.

In March, 1948, after he had left the National Film Board, he wrote in *Documentary Film News* (7, No. 63) of *Bronco Busters*:

> For my money, I would have liked to see more of the Royal Show aspect of the Calgary Stampede, with the big Herefords in from the foothills, but the atmosphere is good and ordinary Calgary... and not without a certain reference back to windbreaks and sundry other aspects of progressive farming, which I thought moderately thoughtful on the part of somebody. Maybe it is true that the local idiom in Canada is a trifle corny, but whose idiom is not? Here is fast and sensitive camera-work and good reportage in anybody's language: of the boys from the farm showing their paces at a local agricultural show... and it does not pretend to do any more. When did I last see a film as good about the Bath Show?

The old Motion Picture Bureau's *Ride 'Em, Cowboy* has not only been brought up to date, but the Calgary Stampede has been endowed with new dignity and authority by comparison with the Royal Agricultural Society of England, incorporated in 1840, and the Bath and West.

> *Tomorrow's Citizens* is another, more serious, matter altogether. The task was to produce a serious film editorial for theatres on a world subject: in ten-minute length. To my knowledge, it had never been done before, and represented

an experiment that was important for all of us. Seeing a ten-minute theatre discussion of educational principle and ideology was a very rare bird indeed, not to mention a very literate account of the ever-recurring gap between technological progress and educational substance. I'm damned if I can see, at this stage, how a one-reel editorial form can do otherwise. The tabloid shape tends to be a propaganda shape, and it is true that *Tomorrow's Citizens* hits you on the head and is done with it. It does, in fact, raise one of the most profound problems before education since Marx first posed it in the poverty of philosophy a hundred years ago. It goes to the pains of fitting the subject within a world framework that includes fundamental education, and to the courtesy of including an almost incredible variety of international illustration.

After commenting, and perceptively, on some other films produced after his time, including *Montreal by Night*, "which makes you feel warm about one of the warmest cities in the world," he moves into an analysis of Canada that is memorable:

I have the impression, for instance, that Canada is not very knowledgeable about political philosophy or the law, especially in the higher branches of these disciplines, though on the other hand it is enormously good at economics. It is somewhat crude in parliamentary debate and there are more cockerels crowing on local editorial dunghills than you could conceive outside Lilliput, but on the other hand, it has a remarkable Institute of International Affairs and solid groups of political study in every town in the country.

Its public life lacks courage and Canada is the village that voted the earth was flat, in the denial of its size and destiny. Yet, its carelessness of distance is fantastic and its individual adventures into the Arctic, epic. Its educational standards are in many quarters grotesque.... Yet, the library work, the adult educational developments and the extension services of the voluntary associations are heartening and good.

Canada especially can be a great bore when it tries to match its sophistication with the larger and deeper versions thereof. "Sunset, and evening star and one clear call for Bill

79

the lone fisherman." But over and under these variations and anomalies, there is a profound element of common sense and good taste about Canada and Canadian life which is a precious thing to know. This the Film Board reflects and demonstrates.

The article was titled "O Canada! We stand on Guard for Thee," and some thoughtful consideration might be given to the question of whether his comments were equally applicable to pre-war and post-war Canada, and even to what extent they may be relevant today. But we can assume that the national character, here briefly and brilliantly defined, constituted to a large extent the terms of reference within which he began to work in 1939.

It is not my intention, nor do I have the capacity, to survey the vast diversity of the images of Canada that Grierson brought to the screen. But it is fair to say that when he virtually abolished "scenics," we began to see more clearly.

The first revelation was the imaginative extension of our sense of our geography to secure the apparently boundless north in the orderly pattern of nine provinces arrayed from east to west. James Beveridge, an intuitive geographer by nature, was assigned thousands of feet of footage on the Mackenzie River, a legacy from the Motion Picture Bureau, and successfully contrived, at last, to bring it into shape, a shape more evocative of brave men, intrepid explorers, mighty rivers, inhospitable wastes, and ingeniously simple forms of transport, than could be found in dog-eared school books with their laboured illustrations. Subsequently, *Look to the North*, on sparkling new stock untrammeled by huskies, established a new image of easy command — Canadian men in parkas and steel helmets manouevring massive bulldozers, *Tigers of the North*, *Tearing Wealth from the Earth*, as two Motion Picture Bureau titles would have it.

Alexei Tremblay, Habitant, from Crawley's unit, had some repercussions. Grierson was accused of perpetuating old myths about rural Quebec, but most western Canadians were astounded by the persistent integrity of its values, and perhaps humbled by the insight into French Canada that the film provides. At the time, one might have argued that it had affinities (anthropological) with *Song of Ceylon*. Now we might argue that it anticipated a historian like LaDurie.

Crawley's *Four Seasons in the Gatineau*, and *Four New Apple*

Dishes, are equally memorable, not least in Halifax, Saskatoon, and Winnipeg. The first was sensitive rather than scenic observation, and the second not 'primary products," but an enchanting confirmation of the rôle of the women who fed the children, the farmers, the truck drivers, the bankers, and the civil servants.

Then we had the films on painters, Canadian painters, and the wilderness of lakes, pines, fringed by small, snow-bound villages. These images obliterated the grocers' calendar, the chromolithographs, and G. F. Watts' *Hope*, and substantially provided provincial Canada with a new, if dim, awareness that art might not be beyond our comprehension.

Who will forget *Trans-Canada Express*, sweeping past a silo in Saskatchewan, blowing a mournful whistle ("the loneliest sound in the world"), and swaggering with a great curve of a shot into Halifax, laden with food and ammunition? Or *Wings of a Continent*, the film on civil aviation Grierson had long since determined upon, mischievously evading IATA's injunction never to discuss safety, with a line of commentary commiting us to our future in the air: "TCA — bravest and safest little Airline in the world."

It had long been accepted, often with some resentment, that most of our industry was centred in Ontario, but the coal mines and steel works in the Maritime provinces seemed remote, and their workers a rather mysterious breed apart. When war came, Canada had swiftly to industrialize on an unprecedented scale, and Grierson was anxious to provide films that would most effectively create pride and confidence, and even familiarity with the new plants, new skills, new output. So we had *Chemicals for Canada*, *Smoke and Steel*, and *Men and Machines*, and if the new images of a newly industrialized nation seemed strange to some of us, we were fortunate to have Graham McInnes, who had the old English passion for coal, steam, and iron, to give them local habitation. *Men and Machines* was shot by Donald Fraser with poetic lucidity, equal to the best work of the Shell Film Unit. Grierson always regretted his own inability easily to understand science and technology, and it may not be unfair to say that the "aesthetics of technology" never took root in Canada.

Withal, one might analyze the hundreds of films with which Grierson was associated, and demonstrate that their images were all about work, even the productive chicken in *La Poulette Grise* industriously laying her eggs. Here I would like to make another observation, that he thought no film worth making unless it could be assured the widest possible distribution, to which end he himself worked hard, and engaged the best people he could, to establish an indestructible distribution system, in the theatres, in the rural circuits, in the schools, clubs, libraries, town halls, and in the newsreels.

From the association between Alan Field and an American newsreel team came two of the most gratifyingly sensational images of Canada. By means of a blaring invitation to be on the screen, they assembled every fishing boat on the west coast, and every farmer who owned a combine harvester. Shot from the air, a small British Columbia harbour was teeming with what appeared to be the largest fishing fleet in the world, and a few sections of land on the prairies were replete with more agricultural machinery than one would have thought possible. Memorable images of an underpopulated country in the newsreels of innumerable American cinemas.

After Forsyth Hardy's contribution to this seminar, and his incisive and scholarly biography, it is with some diffidence that I turn to other considerations. Much has been made of Grierson and the pulpit, even of the few shillings he made as a young itinerant preacher. Did he not declare to Ronald Bloomer that he derived his authority from Moses? He was a profoundly reverent man, and if his authority came from the Old Testament, his tender grace came from the New. "In the Beginning was the Word," and he was adamantly opposed to religious films, and to the presumptuous futility of religious images on the screen.

He was, however, quite capable of being confidently opinionated, and apparently off-hand in matters of the spirit. Some years ago, a new scandal rocked England's green and pleasant gardens. Grierson wrote to *Country Life*: "The sods with their bayonets turning! Devil nip me, when I was a child, nobody scampered through a graveyard, much less tore down its tombstones to make crazy paving."

When his godson was baptised, he sent a telegram saying: "When it comes to the bit about the old Adam leaving this child, count me out." In due course, the boy was confirmed, and Grierson wrote to him: "Dear Charles, Your mother is a great one for calling us to our duty, and no let-up. I shall not be at your Confirmation, as your spiritual welfare has never kept me awake, nor is it ever likely to. But I would like to say that I hope you look up in the College Chapel...that its rich architecture stays with you for the rest of your life, and that you stay faithfully by the priest or parson, as he may be, unless you have other medicine men on hand. If, however, you become a great artist, you will need neither priest, parson, nor medicine man. But this notion will not have escaped you."

We are prone to forget what a good listener he was. On hearing a quotation (source now forgotten) that in Shakespeare's time, there was a solemn bass of mystery and religion, to which each man played his own descant, he was silent and thoughtful. What we are attempting to define, and will be attempting for a very long time to come, is the quality of descant Grierson played in his lifetime. Perhaps it was more quiet than we remember.

Quite properly, there has been much discussion about Grierson *qua* teacher, and most of us are familiar with his theories of education, not least since Hardy's admirable *Grierson on Documentary*, both editions. Hardy also found, among the papers in a chicken coop or wood shed at Tog Hill, Grierson's declaration that an educator ought to take a Hippocratic oath.

It may well be time to put aside many of his oft-quoted remarks about hammers and pulpits and even the creative treatment of actuality, and look for the consistency in his teaching, the emphasis on the continuity of crafts, skills, communities, families, totems, and even cooking. (I have a letter that begins: "To make good Minestrone, you must begin with Marxist principles.") It is possible that scholars in French-speaking Canada might best undertake a study of this kind, for Grierson is closer to Mark Bloch, Fernand Braudel, and Les Annalistes than the rest of us realize.

Perhaps inevitably, he was the kind of teacher who attracted a lyceum, even in a pub, and if one dare so put it, like Socrates, St. Paul, the Venerable Bede, or Snorri Sturlaugsson. He had, I think, few affinities with Matthew Arnold, Richard Hoggart, or Marshall McLuhan. Unexpectedly, he did not dwell over-long on the excellence of the Scottish Academies, and liked to think of himself as one of the light-keepers from whom he descended. He was inordinately proud of their literacy, but if the white rose of Scotland pricked his heart, it was in his irrational hatred of second-hand or public-library books. This, I may say primly, cost the rest of us a pretty penny. But what light-keeper is not worth it?

What is to be done? Two Grierson archives have been established, not without imagination, effort, and finance, and who is going to use them, and for what? As an uneasy trans-Atlantic person, I have misgivings about the North American addiction to tape, not yet an acknowledged research tool for Europeans. Yes, of course, Tennyson reading a poem, but not the whole of *Mein Kampf* roared out by its author. We have, as Grierson said of McLuhan, to sort out the good ideas from the bad, and consider the shape and direction of the archive here.

I have suggested a detailed study of Grierson's theories of education, as published in his essays, or transcribed from the tapes, which could be backed up by that which is both explicit and implicit in his films. Ideally, a study of this kind ought to be undertaken in the light of contemporary educational theory.

It goes without saying that for any scholar other than a pure cinéast in the vast field of communications studies, film, as Grierson deployed it, must be considered in conjunction with newspapers and journals, radio, and television. Canada is more vulnerable in these matters than most countries, and students ought to be concerned with the implications of the Kent Report, the persistent responsibility of the Canadian Broadcasting League, and the tangled cables of the television networks. How well Hugo McPherson put it (*Maclean's*, 16 June 1980).

Those most absorbed by the Grierson legacy might pursue the study of the images he confirmed, embellished, created, or even fabricated, but not without an examination of the post-Grierson imagery in relation to Canadian social, political, economic, educational, and cultural needs. An art historian might want to examine his iconography in the light of his broad knowledge of painting, and his awareness of the response of artists to the economics of their patronage (a response he insisted upon at the Film Board).

His insistence that his McGill students ought to begin with Plato had a comic aspect in the 1940s, but it is nearly impossible to infer from his film-making his formidable intellectual resources. Plato, of course, and the Bible, Kant, Cervantes, Swift, Dostoyevsky, Joyce, Wells, Neibuhr, Yeats, and e. e. cummings, and in his last years, Lévi-Strauss. The concept of *bricollage* gave him immense pleasure. I think back rather lamely to a brief, compressed example of his ability to relate an image and a thesis — a postcard he sent me from Venice, which he thought the most beautiful city in the world, with a view of the interior of the Doge's Palace. On the back of the postcard he had written: "A considered answer to Veblen?"

God was in his head and in his understanding, if not always in his tongue and in his speaking. He never wrote a bad sentence in his life, for he was a good and faithful servant of the word, with a

84

reverence for language that gives his writing and his thinking some kind of indisputable authority.

His summing-up was characteristically understated: "The story of the documentary movement is in part the story of how, not without a scar or two, we got by." If we pursue the story to the end, we might find a "Truth More First than Sun, More Last than Stars," but we would do him a disservice if we thought that he was its "onlie begetter."

H. FORSYTH HARDY

Democracy as a Fighting Faith

A FEW YEARS before his death, John Grierson made a film with me called *I Remember, I Remember*. He took the title from Thomas Hood's poem. He was thinking about his origins, "The house where I was born," but not, I imagine, of "The little window where the sun / Came peeping in at morn." The sun wouldn't have come peeping in anyway. Grierson would have been up to greet it.

If you are to understand Grierson and the direction his life took, you have to understand the forces that influenced his boyhood and upbringing and that remained with him as he wandered over the world. His parents were teachers, dedicated to their profession to a degree one seldom finds today, even in Scotland, with its long tradition in education. His father was headmaster of the local school, a man of stature, respected, even revered, in the community. If a pupil needed the tawse at school the pupil's father, out of respect for the headmaster's judgment, would see that the boy got a second belting at home in the evening. Grierson's mother was a gentler soul and considered by many the better teacher. She came from a suffragette background and her concern for the welfare of the community went far beyond educational attainment in the classroom. When I met her her eye was still bright and her mind razor-sharp — qualities we found again in her large family.

For Grierson, therefore, education, as we knew it in Scotland in the first decade of the century, was a way of life. For him, as with the other members of his family, it was inconceivable that they should not go on to the university. It is significant that they chose to go to Glasgow rather than Edinburgh. As some of you know, Stirling lies roughly equidistant between the two cities. The village where Grierson grew up, on the outskirts of Stirling, was part industrial, part farming. Most of the village men were miners, and the hardships of the miner's life had been seen at first hand by the

86

young Grierson. He had helped in the soup kitchens organized by his mother to relieve distress in the village during strikes.

Something of the injustice inherent in their treatment stuck with him. It pushed him towards the Socialist party then emerging in Scotland under the leadership of Keir Hardie. The experience of growing up in a mining village gave him the background for a film he made many, many years later, *The Brave Don't Cry.*

The other dominant influence of Grierson's early life was the sea. His family came from a long line of light-keepers. One of the very first names entered in copper-plate in the leather-bound record books of the Commissioners of Northern Lighthouses in Edinburgh is JOHN GRIERSON, one of his progenitors. His father had been brought up among fishermen in the small village of Boddam near Peterhead. Grierson himself spent many of his holidays in lighthouses. He was in one such lighthouse in August, 1914, at the beginning of World War One, and watched the trawlers and drifters returning to become mine-sweepers and anti-submarine patrols. A love of the sea was deeply implanted in him. It was inevitable, therefore, that when he was accepted for war service, by misrepresenting his age, he opted for the navy. It was equally natural that when he made his first film many years later it should be of ships and the seas.

In *Drifters* you have a meeting of those two influences I have been identifying in Grierson's life, education and the sea. Before that film was made, of course, many things had happened. There was his return, after the war, to Glasgow University and his closer involvement in the Socialist movement, itself a reflection of the social upheaval of the post-war period. One of the great revolutionary fighters of that time in Scotland was John McLean who, because of his views, spent several periods in prison, the last on a hunger strike. Grierson never forgot seeing him emerge, a broken man. He confessed many years later to having burst into tears at the sight. Experiences of this kind in what was known as the Red Clyde left a permanent mark on him. Later he was to say, "What I may have given to documentary — with the working man on the screen and all that — was simply what I owed to my masters, Keir Hardie, Bob Smillie, and John Wheatley."

The other big thing that happened was his visit to the United States. In Chicago, a dynamic city then, as now, he was conscious of the turbulent flow of immigrants and the complex problem of communication they presented. The yellow press, with its direct translation of event into active headlines, pointed to the first solution. It was Walter Lippmann who turned him towards the cinema, with its immense and ever widening range of communication. His studies in Hollywood gave him an understanding well ahead of his time of what could be said in films, and to whom. He may have been living in the world of Clara Bow and Thelma Todd (whom he claimed to have discovered); but he was thinking a little more deeply about how the fact of life could be dramatized and interpreted for the good of the public and the betterment of their life.

So, as I have said, *Drifters* was the outcome. It was his first opportunity to give expression not only to the influences of his upbringing but also to those that were shaping his adult life. Here was a film about the sea. Here was a film about man and his environment. Here was a film that escaped from the artificiality of studio drama and portrayed life as it was. As yet no social criticism. It was enough of a break with tradition for a film to be concerned with the every-day world of the working man. *Drifters* should be evaluated not in contemporary terms, where its achievement would scarcely register in television's flow of actuality, but as a revolutionary departure in its day. For Grierson it meant opening doors, laying foundations, taking initiatives — all the things he was to spend the rest of his life doing.

It was never easy, this inserting of social purpose into the cinema. One of my abiding memories of Grierson in the thirties is of him travelling all over Britain, firing audiences large and small with his visionary enthusiasm. He was, until the end of his life, an inspiring speaker who could make an audience believe in his message and send them away determined to do something about it. What we didn't see was the struggle to get his ideas accepted at Whitehall. The British government was still nervous about the persuasive power of the cinema. Each new film embodying criticism of social conditions — on housing, nutrition, health, the environment — was regarded somewhat apprehensively. Grierson enlisted the aid of the newspapers and the enlightened journalists of his day to help to create the atmosphere for acceptance.

I remember how the issue came into the open at the time of the New York World's Fair in 1938. Grierson had been adviser on a group of six films about Scotland — a modest but, at that time, a remarkably comprehensive view of a country, its agriculture, industry, fishing, education, health, recreation, and way of life. In these films Grierson was free of any narrow sponsor restriction and could go as deep and as wide as he liked. The warts were there. Those who were selecting the films to go to the British pavilion in New York did not like the warts. They didn't select the films. Grierson went into action and had the newspapers solidly behind him. The Whitehall establishment stood firm. The battle for authenticity was called "knee breeches or working clothes." The films *were* shown in New York, under American auspices. In the calm after the battle, Grierson reflected: "It has taken a good deal of persistence to maintain that a full and true story of British life is more likely to describe our virtues as a democracy, and that the richest picture to present in Britain and other countries lies in the actual bone and substance of British life."

Grierson and his associates got as near as they could to the bone and substance of British life by the end of the decade that had seen the birth of the documentary movement. They were still working under the handicap of the absence of total government commitment to the use of film. In health, education, and labour a beginning had been made but there was no overall guiding purpose. It seemed as if all the potential Grierson had been developing in men and ideas was being stultified. In fairness, it should be remembered that the times were difficult. It wasn't easy to look forward confidently at the time of the Munich crisis and the rape of Czechoslovakia. Grierson himself always thought positively.

When Grierson moved to Canada in 1939, the restrictions that had hampered his ambitions for the social use of film fell away. Here was a new country, a clean slate. Here above all — once the groundwork had been done — was the commitment of a government, coming from the top. It was as if he could do for Canada, with a long perspective, what he had done in a small way, with a limited objective and a limited budget, for Scotland.

We can see that most clearly if we think only of the two series of films: "Canada Carries On" — "what Canadians need to know and think about if they are going to do their best by Canada and themselves;" and "World in Action" — "concerned primarily with the relation of local strategies to larger world ones." How rewarding it must have been for him to be able to move freely in an area of communication, where previously in Britain he had known restriction and reluctance!

I speak about how it looked from the other side. How did it appear to Grierson? In the spring of 1942 Grierson had what his doctors called a heart attack — he called it "a silly species of exhaustion." He was sent off for a rest to Sarasota, in Florida. He didn't rest. He began by writing long letters to his friends. Chief among them was his old chief, Sir Stephen Tallents.

"The film thing," he wrote to him, "has now the appearance of being deeply founded in Canada, with all the ordinary marks of success, for what they are worth. Our films have broken through the American market and a lot of the critics are hailing them as the best war films from anywhere so far. In some ways I think they may be, at least in the deliberation of their propaganda plan. There has been a great deal of thought and research behind the films and of a more deliberate and scientific nature than we ever got organized in England. They have acquired a certain present pertinence and size from considering the more far-reaching and difficult patterns of the war. The world strategy of food, for example, which goes back in a curious way to the EMB and John Orr, but less sentimental than Orr. We have certainly diverged a long way from the documentary model now being pursued in England: in the direction of more knowledge of political plan and the design behind the news."

You will sense in that, therefore, Grierson's own assessment of what he had been able to do in Canada, in comparison with his achievement in Britain. He was writing with discretion, as one public servant to another. The Canadians, he continued, had taken it all very well.

> We have a crew of nearly two hundred now and it's a good crew with plenty of energy and goodwill and the footloose atmosphere in which they work is a minor wonder, and achievement, for Ottawa. I would like to think it is a sign of hope in Canada itself and not just the result of the skill in manoeuvre I got from you. Unfortunately, we haven't discovered yet enough people of first-rate power to hold down the wide field we are being progressively given. Two and perhaps three series of films — they are all worked in series — have really good personnel behind them. The others slide and slip in only relative competence and it's a problem to know how to give the natively not-so-good the kind of production approach that lets a producer sleep easily at nights.

We have now as many as seventy films on the stocks at one time, and of all sorts and kinds. Legg has emerged as the most powerful news editor and commentator in films in North America, but we could do with half a dozen of him. We have our political worries too, because the limelight which now shines on us, particularly from the States, makes its inevitable quota of enemies. Some quarters in Washington are none too happy because we have been used by the New York press as an example, in criticism of their own local efforts; and, of course, their situation is quite different and more difficult with more inevitable red tape to wade through. Poor Washington is a dreadful place to work in: so self-complicated, so rich in individualist talents and little plan or faith to hold them in co-operation and unity. Canada is, thank heaven, smaller and, I suppose because everybody knows everybody else, you can keep things from dying or dimming in a welter of formalism.

I am not going to say any more by way of comparing the film situation under Grierson in Britain and Canada. There are others in this audience who can speak for Canada. I certainly think of what Grierson was able to do at the National Film Board as a model of what can be achieved by a determined, clear-sighted man under a liberal-minded administration in a young country, growing fast and still making exciting discoveries about its strengths and capacities. I think of the documentary movement that he founded in Britain taking a new lease on life in Canada, being born again, if you like. He seized the opportunity Mackenzie King gave him. Canada gained greatly. And documentary, too.

Margaret tells me that, while they were in Sarasota, at a place called Midnight Pass, Grierson spent the forenoon writing, the afternoon fishing, and the evening drinking. The perfect combination, I imagine, for him. He had been commissioned by a London publisher to write a book to be called *Eyes of Democracy*, and the forenoon sessions were spent on it. In the month he was in Florida, nominally resting, he wrote about sixty thousand words and prepared notes on the remainder. He never did have the time or the peace of mind to complete it. Eventually he wrote to the publisher, withdrawing from the contract on the pretext that "directors of information [he was then manager of the Wartime Information

Board] should not write books while they are directors of information ... my written views are too sharply put for this young nation to take easily."

I found the uncompleted manuscript among Grierson's papers while I was researching for the biography. It has never seen the light of day and you are the first audience to hear any of it. I am going to give you only a comparatively short passage from the opening chapter. I give you it because it reflects Grierson's thinking at a key moment in his life and because it embodies some of the points I have been making about the documentary movement.

I have been a propagandist all my working life because I have believed that we needed to do our democratic mind over if we were going to save democracy. I have believed that in education was the heart of the matter, but that education needed to be revolutionized altogether if it was to become the instrument of revolutionized democracy I was thinking of. I have known it was a long and perplexing journey, and I have often considered that we might not be in time. I have been desperately afraid that we might not be in time, and events have proved my fears sickeningly prophetic. I have accordingly been a man in a hurry, and I will confess now that being in a hurry in the English thirties was a despairing line of business. As far as a man may, I have organized my own educational revolution, and that is what the documentary movement is and what it is about.

I chose films because they got to more people. I chose the documentary idea because it fitted the democratic conception and could get me closer to the people and events that my fighting democracy was about; but it had the special advantage of being cheap and within my power to finance. I have had to pretend to a whole lot of powers I didn't have in running my education revolution. I have had to be a creative worker and a civil servant and a promoter and an organizer and a critic and a teacher of the youth; and, though I hate finance and know nothing about it, I have had to find the millions, often from people whom I dared not tell fully what I was after lest it would seem pretentious. It would have sounded silly if I had said:

"I am not really a promoter or an organizer or a critic and I could only weep in humility if you called me a creative

92

worker, but, by God, I am a fighting believer in democracy, and you are perverting it and whittling it away and bringing it to disaster, and the time is short, and I want your money to teach as many people as I can and as fast as I can the patterns of thought and feeling that will make democracy real, and because more real, more worthy to fight for and more sure to survive." It would have been silly to say that I wanted democracy on the offensive again lest it die for a lifetime, when I was talking in a complacent world that believed all too much in its infinite righteousness and infinite security and hated the idea of democracy on the offensive because democracy involved sacrifice and it was unwilling to sacrifice. I can say it now because at last I have the facts of the four freedoms with me "everywhere in the world."

The documentary movement may not seem much, but it came true, for all efforts, conscious and unconscious, to detach it from the idea and whittle away its intention have failed. It has proved happily that it could not be tempted into money or respectability or even into art. But there is nothing surprising about that, because a need of the times was with it and the young men who developed it were sick of the complacency and futility into which the democratic process was slipping, and like good men everywhere were willing to serve their generation as they knew best. The documentary movement may not be much but it illustrates, I think, where the conception of a revitalized democracy leads.

It involves research into the patterns of thought which are developing. It demonstrates how new sentiments can be crystalized by dramatic medium. It points the way to a new conception of education. It shows how the educational instrument in the hands of a nation can be made a creative instrument of democracy's leadership. It reveals how even a complex industrial civilization can be centrally planned and organized without taking away from the people the sense of the actuality of understanding it and willing it a fresher participation in it and, out of it, participant citizenship controlling it. It is in that sense one way of indicating how democracy can be made to work and achieve, and just as vitally and just as creatively as any slick and enslaving system which the Devil and the Grand Inquisitor can devise.

This may be some indication of good reason to those I have pestered and high-pressured and bullied and beaten and perhaps hurt like an hoodlum in getting my job done. Long ago when I lived in Chicago and observed the ways of the Chicago gangsters, it seemed a pity that there should be systems of protection for everybody except artists. I have also never forgotten a word which John Wheatley spoke to me: "Never get into a fight, especially a political fight, unless you are prepared to defend yourself." If the documentary movement stands alone as the only movement of free and independent workers which has survived in the history of the movies, it is because it has hitched its wagon to a systematic and necessary idea and has kept it hitched; but it is also because it has known that growth involved the violence of a growing point and that the best form of defence is attack. The form of its protective system in England is, I sometimes think, very pretty indeed and strange for a group of artists to organize; but then again, the art came out of the idea and the idea could not at any cost afford defeat.

I have, of course, been paraded at various times as an uncomfortable character for a public servant to be, and certainly I have always fought my battles as though I intended to win them.

Grierson was a fighter in all and everything he did, as this passage I have quoted demonstrates. In the earliest photograph I have of him he has a black eye. He was never happier in his life than when he was bombarding complacency. Let us not be complacent about any of the issues we discuss here in his name.

COLIN LOW

Grierson and Challenge for Change

DR. GRIERSON had a love-hate relationship with the "Challenge for Change" program. One got the feeling that he sincerely hoped it would succeed but was sure that it would fail.

He had always talked about the "teacher/film-maker," the "educator/film-maker." He conceded that these people should also be blessed with artistry and wisdom. He tried to preach these people into existence.

Here, in the late sixties, in this Film Board program, were a few energetic, naïve enthusiasts who, for a short time, believed again that it was possible to change the world with the camera.

That excited Grierson. They were teachers, social workers, film-makers, and they were not only prepared to teach with film, they were also prepared to help ordinary people to make their own films. That bothered Grierson. That was carrying things too far.

In late 1971 I had three encounters with Dr. Grierson that were illuminated by his exasperation with the program.

I was just emerging from five years of "Challenge for Change." The Fogo Island project, which became a cornerstone of that program, was like one of those events in science where conditions come together and seem to prove something fundamental. But then, try and duplicate the results in another laboratory! I was still defending the Fogo approach as not only practical, but essential.

For those people now who have never heard of the Fogo Island project — and there will be many who have not — I will put it in a nutshell. I used to take much longer to describe it. It was a community-development program in Newfoundland, well-planned and well-funded, which used film as a catalyst to generate local debate — to give local people a voice and even an editorial control — and to provide those people with access to people in power, via film. Not one film but a whole series of mini-films. It was meant to be a

95

step in incorporating media into the democratic process. The creation of a communication loop, as we called it. All of these are things one can imagine Dr. Grierson applauding. It seemed to work. It seemed to foster positive, creative social change. But there has never been any way of proving that film caused the change. Later projects substantiated the approach. Few were quite as dramatic.

Fourteen years later, Fogo Island is one of the healthier communities in Newfoundland, and we can't say for sure why it is that way.

Grierson referred to his McGill class at that time as a "very promising group" of young teachers. He had weeded them out of a much larger group because he was fed up with film groupies and dilettantes, he said.

They were the *crème de la crème* and he wanted me to talk to them about "community," and would I bring some film to run?

I thought I could do this with my eyes shut. I had done it a dozen times before. I picked three films with not much thought. Oddly enough, apart from social gatherings, where I had felt very comfortable in his presence, this was the first time I saw Grierson on his professional ground as a teacher.

He looked small and fragile when he arrived, but his looks were deceiving. He first of all berated one of the very large, bearded, long-haired students for putting his foot on a seat in Theatre Six at the Film Board. It was a seat that many feet had been applied to, in the course of fifteen years, but I gathered that Dr. Grierson did not appreciate such a lack of formality in his class. By the time he had finished he had everyone's attention, including mine. I must say, at this point I started to worry.

He then launched into a recapitulation of the previous lecture, which had to do with his experience working as a reporter for the Hearst Press in Chicago — and his interest in yellow journalism for its active and dramatic method of arresting popular attention. The expression "something does something to something" was used to illustrate the idea of the kind of story-telling in such dramatic journalism. Such headlines as AIRPLANE HITS HILL illustrated the device. Not AIRPLANE CRASHES ON HILL.

From there he went on to indicate that he had tried to apply some of these ideas to documentary film, to galvanize interest in large political, social, economic issues, in the conviction that the man in the street could be interested, and involved, and participate in shaping the world.

He also sketched the growth of fascist propaganda-film and pointed out some of the differences between democratic media and fascist media, as expressed in wartime and peacetime situations, but always emphasizing the dramatic.

I had been much impressed by reading Dr. Grierson's ideas on the general sanction of Parliament as applied to the National Film Board: the idea that, as a film-maker, one had to respect the constraints as well as the possibilities of this sanction. I had used the paragraph to influence film-makers in "Challenge for Change" who had resorted to very subjective and emotional positions in the expression of situations in films.

At this point Dr. Grierson began to emphasize the importance of expression, personal style, passion, poetry, as important elements in the documentary. He then introduced me and made some very positive remarks about the style and expression of some of my films. Unfortunately, they were not the films I was about to show. I showed a film called *The Hutterites*, done long before the "Challenge for Change" program, my first experience of trying to bridge the gap between a remote and unusual community and the outside world.

Dr. Grierson hated it. He saw the Hutterites as essentially antisocial, and the style of the film as pedestrian. His critique was devastating.

My colleagues at the NFB had been critical of the film when it was completed because it did not highlight the serious conflict between the Hutterites and their western materialist neighbours. They said it was too pals-y with the Hutterites. It was not dramatic enough for television.

I had argued with them that there would never be a decent discussion between the Hutterites and their neighbours until there was some common base of good-will and mutual respect, and part of that was being able to show the minority group as unique, but admirable, folks. Highlighting the tensions on TV was not going to contribute to community peace.

But I didn't know what to say to Dr. Grierson. Here was a man who had told us in the forties that our task was to make peace more exciting than war. I had brought him my film to praise for its sincere effort, and he had ripped it to shreds. "In a film you must tell a story," he said, "otherwise you are boring, you will not have an audience. Something *does* something *to* something. You must reveal the secret inside of that interaction, whether it is a psychological story, a political story, or a story about tying shoe-laces."

I sulked at the side of the theatre. "But, but," I protested silently in my own head. "In a community the best story is the peaceful and collaborative solution of problems. That is not theatre. The best community development is evolutionary, not revolutionary. Why is that not an exciting story? Do people have to hang on the edge of survival in order to be interesting? Is accommodation more ignoble than a western shoot-out? Haven't we had enough of that media crap?"

"We'll now look at the next film," said Dr. Grierson.

I wished I was in another city. I ran the film *Billy Crane*, a Fogo Island fisherman who, that day, was pulling up his nets to leave and go to Toronto to work in a factory. It is a monologue — a quiet, bitter, unstructured verbal ramble.

Dr. Grierson liked Billy Crane. He didn't think much of the film but he pointed out Billy Crane's verbal skill and dramatic flair in story-telling — his superb timing and phrasing, the pauses, the punctuation of his thinking with little actions. He suggested that many local people have a great oral tradition, an untutored but superb command of language in its essence.

I started to relax. I wanted to say that the film had been most important for our work and had been received initially with shock and then with enthusiasm. The provincial government had a hard time answering Billy Crane. But they did answer him. I wanted to say that this *"giving a voice to people"* was what it was all about, but I was too late.

"What," Dr. Grierson wanted to know, "was the value of the film off Fogo Island? Was it good for television? Mass media? What did it say to Canada?" I was deflated. "What did it say to the world?"

I had to admit the film wasn't worth much outside the context of the situation — outside the mainland of Newfoundland. Billy Crane's accent was hard to understand. It had some specialized value in Ottawa, but it did not say much to farmers in Alberta, except that centralization and central decisions of government are not necessarily always right.

"How can you afford to make expensive films for such a limited clientèle? Why would the Canadian tax-payer allow such an indulgence?" Dr. Grierson asked.

I pointed out that we recognized the cost but that it was experimental, and the whole project — twenty-seven films for local use —

cost less than one CBC television hour at current costs. Now I was fighting back. "Besides," I said, "welfare in any depressed area was expensive, but if development was accomplished — "

"Twenty-seven films for local, limited consumption!" Dr. Grierson interrupted. "Did any of these films define the problems, and recommend solutions to the problems of the island?" Grierson wanted to know.

"Well, no," I said. "The films were an effort to help the community define its own solutions, by playing back their tentative efforts of formulation. Video equipment and tape were also useful, and cheaper than film."

"So the film-maker is nothing but a tool, a camera operator or projectionist in the formulation of these problems and solutions. What about the intelligence, world experience, expensive education that could be brought to these people? If you have no opinions, no ideas, no commitments, nothing to say, why further burden these poor folks, whose lives are difficult enough, with manipulative nonsense? They need all their working energy and time to simply get by."

At this point I caved in temporarily. I said I often had the same questions in my head on Fogo Island but that honestly I could not recommend anything to these people. Their situation, which seemed to me initially simple, became more and more complex as I learned more and more about them. We were working with a community development man from Memorial University on Fogo. The university supplied the hard information on many subjects; I supplied the film know-how. I think I blurted out that a lot of documentary films are simply massive oversimplifications of reality.

Dr. Grierson looked profoundly skeptical. I felt barely conscious as I walked out the door. "We haven't finished," said Dr. Grierson, "Come back next week. I think you've got another film. Oh! Better book the theatre."

Next week Dr. Grierson asked me to tell the class about the film we were going to see. My remarks were succinct. This is what I said:

"At the height of Kennedy's famous war on poverty, a one-and-a-half-billion-dollars-a-year agency called the Office of Economic Opportunity in Washington heard about the Fogo Island experiment. Subsequently a number of similar experiments were conducted in the United States: the Farmersville project in California; the Hartford project in Connecticut; the Sky River project in Alaska; the White House report on hunger. All modelled after Fogo. Altogether several million dollars of effort.

"*Hector and Reuben* is an interview with two young, Spanish-American war veterans. The war was Vietnam; they had just returned. Their father and mother were illegally-entered Spanish-Americans — agricultural workers, orange pickers, in a town called Farmersville, California. The town was a tinderbox of racial resentment. The film did a great deal to start the two sides talking. Washington was impressed."

We ran the film for Dr. Grierson's class, as I will run it for you now....

After the screening, Dr. Grierson asked the class what they thought about the film.

Some of the class were American conscientious objectors, including the big guy with long hair whom Dr. Grierson had mauled a week before in the foot-on-the-seat incident. The opinions of the class were mixed. Some thought Hector and Reuben were telling the interviewer what he wanted to hear. Some saw in the cautious discussion only embarrassment. Some saw in it subservience.

"Brown Uncle Tomism" was the phrase. One student thought that anyone who fired a gun in Vietnam was criminal.

Other students objected to this interpretation. They thought the boys had guts. The discussion became very heated.

"The film was a catalyst," I protested. "Only these two boys, who had served in the army, in a town dominated by American white war veterans of three wars, could possibly broach the subject of racism." I felt that in a polarized situation teetering on the edge of violence, someone had to make the gesture, but it could not have the implication of threat.

"One must try to generate a base of good-will," I said, "before any discussions can begin. This kind of medium is totally different from mass media, and this is what is driving me crazy about Dr. Grierson's interpretation."

Dr. Grierson objected, "Not all human situations can be solved without conflict. Good-will is not enough. Do not get confused with sentimentality. Intelligence and strategy are at the heart of diplomacy. You cannot achieve peace out of love and wishful thinking alone.

"Furthermore, the film is ambiguous. It is not an affirmation of love or Christianity. It is not a real service to the subject of the film. It uses them but does it support them with evidence? Evidence, proof: *that* is what you must bring to the situation if you are to be these people's advocate." At this point I stopped being resentful and defensive, and tried to listen. But it was the end of the class.

In the last of the three classes the following week Dr. Grierson recapitulated. I realized, at that point, that he had tricked me.

He knew the answers to all the questions he had asked me. I thought his hostility was genuine — it was his brand of theatre. "Something does something to something" — or to someone. If his students have forgotten the lesson, which I doubt, I have not.

After his death three months later, "Challenge for Change" published in its *Newsletter* his "Memo to Michelle." It expressed his hopes and doubts and faith concerning the decentralization of the means of production. Indeed he hoped it was practical. It was a question of method.

What has happened to "Challenge for Change?" you might ask.

As Dr. Grierson predicted, some of our methods were impracti- -cal. Somewhere in the mid-seventies the program slowly expired — after several attempts to revitalize it — for those reasons Dr. Grierson so deftly fingered in his criticism of the program.

"Evidence." That's what you must bring to these situations — and what you must carry away from the situation.

Government wants evidence. Evidence of change. Cost-benefit analysis. As money became tighter — as the idealistic citizen-participation rhetoric of the sixties did a cross-mix to the rhetoric of energy economics, we saw the emergence of another approach. "Something does something to something," in no uncertain terms. Referendums are won by the merchants of hard-sell. The advertising companies *do* their homework, with statistical evidence. For x dollars you reach y people with z impact. They are hard to refute. They have fifty years of advertising theory and practice behind them and a conditioned populace which, if it does not totally believe the message, at least tolerates it. Repetition does wonders in blurring skepticism. But does that approach to social change alter anything for long?

I could not have acted differently if I had fully understood the implications of Dr. Grierson's message ten years ago. I have faith that the opportunities will return again — and that the methods will be refined by another generation with energy and wisdom.

I cannot forget the actual experience of that program. I am compelled to remember it. Some of our evidence was good, but not always complete.

Those moments when rancour and hostility and anger are transformed by reason and become co-operation and accommodation: I have seen them triggered by an appropriate film. This attitudinal change is hard to get on film, but it is the very root of community. Those moments are hard to record. There are cultures that understand that, in negotiations, people must not be allowed to lose face; they must be able to maintain dignity for the good of the entire community. In Japan this is not theory, this is every-day practice, and there is much to learn in that tradition.

When we ran *Hector and Reuben* for a large Farmersville audience, the Veterans' Hall was packed. The Anglos (white folks) sat on one side of the hall, the Chicanos (brown folks) sat on the other side. When the film was over, an old gentleman with a midwest Oklahoma accent, a former white migrant labourer from the days of *The Grapes of Wrath*, stood up.

"Well," he said, "I appreciated seeing that film and listening to those young men, and I learned something from them. I've got a good Spanish-speaking friend in this town. I've known him for twenty years but I honestly have to admit we don't talk about much except the weather."

His friend across the hall hesitantly stood up and said, "Yes, that's true. We don't talk about much except the weather, and maybe we're both too old to be interested in other things, but why is it not possible for our children to talk about other things?"

It was one of those moments. I might have turned the camera on, I might have got the ensuing discussion, which went on quietly for an hour. But I don't think it would have happened. Is it possible there is some evidence outside the witness of the camera?

No, I don't think the experience and ideas of "Challenge for Change" were impractical.

Our world is impractical. This is a watershed of history. Violence as a method of social problem-solving is now impractical.

At one time a tribal skirmish might have been ugly and brutal, or heroic and exhilarating, necessary or unnecessary depending on what side you were on. It only affected those two tribes.

Violence is impractical because geography, space, and nature no longer contain small violence. Now, what is one day a remote tribal skirmish is next day the *cause célèbre* for a super-power or the invasion of larger vested interest. Instantaneous media do not seem to calm the nervous trigger-fingers, they exacerbate alarm. But we know that it is either a question of co-operation and accommodation or annihilation on a global scale.

No, the ideas of that program were not impractical, Dr. Grierson. Too early, too late, or too little, perhaps.

If we cannot improve our local, regional, and national communication — if we cannot improve the quality of our own community dialogue, how can we walk with any authority upon a world stage and change the nature of that desperate argument?

BASIL WRIGHT

An Innocent in Canada

SEEING SO MANY OLD FRIENDS, some I've not laid eyes on for thirty years, I should like to greet them, and ask them to forgive any inaccuracies.

I worked in Canada with the National Film Board twice during the war, but Grierson used me in a way peculiar to himself, and that makes it not so easy to explain. Jack Ellis talked about what happened at the beginning of the war. From the point of view of the British, what happened was extremely important because we had assumed automatically that Grierson would return and take charge of informational films, if not the whole of information.

When the war broke out, he was on this side of the Atlantic, and nothing happened. It was the period of the phony war, and the so-called Ministry of Information was being run by hard-nosed, soft-headed Conservative bureaucrats who were determined to do nothing to help the war effort. They also put out a memorandum to all government departments saying that everybody in documentary was a communist, that most people in documentary were running companies that were nothing less than bucket shops, and that they had got no financial backing at all.

So we were ostracized as a group, and only saved finally by a generous grant from the Rockefeller Foundation. That kept us on our feet until Hitler's invasion of Europe and the arrival of Churchill.

Churchill appointed Brendan Bracken to the Ministry of Information and Jack Beddington, from Shell Film Unit, to take charge of films. Jack Beddington's first act, on becoming head of the Films Division, was to request a paper from Film Centre, for a fee, explaining how to use films in time of war. Arthur Elton, Edgar Anstey, and I wrote this document and Beddington kept it in the top drawer of his desk throughout the war for constant reference.

So Grierson didn't come back, nor was he invited back. It is my opinion, however, that he expected to be invited. He was at the time travelling to Canada, Australia, and New Zealand for the Imperial Relations Trust. Time went by, and nothing happened.

He began to listen to the Canadian government who decided, since he had drafted a bill to set up a government film unit, that the bill should become an act. Grierson was then invited to be the first commissioner of the National Film Board, and that was really having your cake and eating it too. Just imagine, you draw up a bill, avoiding all the mistakes you've made in your previous work, and then it's handed to you on a plate to administer.

Grierson was very cautious. He agreed to accept for three months. I think he still believed that the British would invite him back. They were mad, of course, not to do so, but that is past history. So, we have him starting from scratch with a full government film unit.

Prime Minister Mackenzie King was very much sold on Grierson. So what does Grierson do? He imports Stuart Legg and Stanley Hawes from England. He must have a couple of lieutenants with experience, because the people he is recruiting are inexperienced.

Now, Grierson had an incredible nose for talent. He would meet kids, boys or girls, sit up and talk to them all night and, before they knew where they were, they'd find themselves either right out in the street or in an old saw-mill in Ottawa at the corner of John and Sussex, which is where the Film Board first started operations. He got together a group of people very quickly, and he made few, if any, mistakes in his choices.

He knew how to play politics also. He lived on the paradoxical, the unexpected. In my long years of friendship with him, I got to recognize his genius of argument, in which he kept reversing rôles. He made replies exactly opposite to what his opponent expected or intended.

At one time in 1943, I was in Winnipeg with Grierson and Ross McLean, who was by then a close friend, to attend a dinner in honour of Dr. J.W. Dafoe, the genius of the *Winnipeg Free Press*, on the occasion of his retirement. A number of speeches were made, including one by Grierson. Dafoe, when he replied, naturally referred to each of the speakers. Of Grierson, he said, "Whenever I see John Grierson, he is galloping past the liberal position in one direction or another."

Grierson started an enormous program of films, but he kept

looking back towards the British Isles, not unnaturally, and he came to the conclusion that the English wartime film effort, however well intentioned, was too slow and too soft. He used to write about this in no uncertain terms, and we often published his letters as unsigned editorials in our own paper, *Documentary News Letter*.

It's perhaps a little known newspaper, *Documentary News Letter*, but it had an extraordinarily surprising influence among governmental departments. You would go to a government department to discuss a film project, or something of that sort, and, as often as not, you'd see on the man's desk a copy of *Documentary News Letter*, tabbed with one of those red things that meant "Urgent this day — do not delay. Deal with it." When you saw that, you felt a little stronger in the negotiations.

Grierson was irked by what he felt was an ignorance of Canada on the part of the British civil service. He noted that the British were still colonially minded, and lumped Canada together with all the other pink blobs on the wall. Eventually, he decided to do something about it, and, for some unearthly reason, he got in touch with Jack Beddington and asked if I could be loaned to the National Film Board. I was not a party to the negotiations.

Now Grierson and Beddington had a wonderful love/hate relationship. Beddington hated all the National Film Board films. He thought they were absolutely frightful. Grierson admired, in a qualified way, the Crown Film Unit productions like *Western Approaches*, and some of the Jennings films, but he felt that the British documentary people worked so slowly and sought such perfection that, by the time the film they were making was finished, there was no further need for it. This irritated him. The British were irritated equally by the fact that, having lavished all the aesthetic intelligence they possibly could on a film like Humphrey Jennings' *Listen to Britain*, one of the most beautiful and undateable films I know, they would discover that it was being hacked to pieces by Stuart Legg, and jammed into a thing called *Canada Carries On*.

So there was a bit of business on both sides. Beddington resisted Grierson's request for me a long time, but eventually agreed that I should go to Canada for four weeks.

So I was shoved onto a flying boat, and made an illegal entry into Canada in the middle of the war. The flying boat came to a place called Shediac, of which I'd never heard, and a man in a rowing boat came out to take me ashore. Then he rented a dilapidated cab to take me to Moncton. I rang Ottawa, and Grierson arranged for me to come there on the next plane. I was pretty bewildered, but presumably not half so bewildered as the RCMP, because, from their point of view, I had never arrived in Canada, nor been through customs, nor had my passport examined. Still, after all, I thought, I've never been here before, perhaps that's how they go on.

My arrival in Ottawa was an emotional moment. There were Grierson and his gorgeous wife, Margaret, and Stuart Legg, and Stanley Hawes, and a host of other people who became fast friends. Many of them are here today.

Grierson seized me by the scruff of the neck, told me to forget everything I'd been doing in England, and to pay close attention to Stuart, who was putting out two lots of films — *World in Action* and *Canada Carries On*. I looked at these in a very startled way because they were made in the *March of Time* style. They were extremely rough, not so much in technical as in ideological terms.

They talked about the war in a way I had not been used to hearing in England. They were looking ahead. The films, through Legg, were studying the political wartime intentions of our enemies with an enormous sort of appreciation. My recollection is that, when the Japanese attacked Pearl Harbour, the Film Board produced a relevant film instantly.

When I was taken to New York, I was thrust into the Warwick Hotel. Here were the people, as Margaret Ann [Elton] has pointed out, who knew the art of distribution, United Artists, and they were all up there in that Warwick penthouse. They were a race of people I'd not met before. I got interested in them and in their method of distribution. The very high pressure of their work made me feel an absolute hick.

What I actually did in Ottawa, I can't really remember. I suppose I talked to all these kids and that would include some of you. Later on, on my way across Canada, I got off at every capital station, bought my liquor (they had rationing), and arrived in Vancouver like a hero. I got a month's ration from Winnipeg, and from all the stations along the line.

These kids showed me their films, their rought cuts. I made comments and suggestions in a rather bruised state because the indoctrination from Grierson and Legg was biting hard.

I was being punched through all the time, and the four weeks went by in a flash. Then I was flung onto a Halifax bomber, given an oxygen mask, and flown to Scotland, appropriately enough. So I went back to my wartime job in London. There was plenty to do. We were very short-staffed because most of our kids had been put in the army.

My next visit in 1943, was altogether different. First of all, Beddington made no objection to loaning me to the National Film Board. He said, "You can have him for six months, if you like," which I thought had got rather an edge to it, sort of, "We can do without him."

So I was taken in great secrecy, unlike the RCMP, to Liverpool and, in great secrecy again, placed on the *Queen Mary*. She could be seen and identified from a distance of about twenty miles and she was decorated with the Dutch colours, and was obviously being used to take Queen Wilhelmina of the Netherlands to the new world to spend the rest of the war.

We were all put under hatches until the ship sailed. When we came up again, there were no more Dutch colours or decorations. Churchill was on board and the general staff, and they were on their way to see President Roosevelt, so we had a rather high-pressure, splendid voyage surrounded by destroyers and submarines and so on.

So there I was, back in the old place again, and being treated with such kindness I can never repay it. Margaret Ann, who was in New York, lent me her apartment, and it was opposite that of Norman McLaren and Guy Glover, two other dear friends.

Tom Daly was wonderful, although he'd fallen off a horse and was in plaster. Still, he treated me with extreme courtesy. I thought I was going to be a producer, but not a bit of it, nothing to do with films. Grierson's idea was to expose me to as many aspects and varieties of Canadian life and thought as possible — political, cultural, economical, and so on, and all this related to the total war effort.

One was hearing those three words constantly in Canada in those days, and in particular at the Film Board. I was being given a travelling scholarship, sort of. Grierson gave me introductions to many influential people, from the true-blue Toronto people to the French in Quebec. Throughout the country I met some wonderful people, and thanks to Tom Daly's parents, I had the privilege of having dinner with A. Y. Jackson. From there, I was led through what was hitherto unknown to me, the fascination and brilliance of the different schools of Canadian art, and to individual geniuses like David Milne.

Eventually Grierson said, "Here is your itinerary." I was to go across the prairies, to Edmonton, into the Northwest Territories, and down to Vancouver. Also, for some reason, I was to go to Hollywood to lecture on how to write scripts.

Now I've never in my life been able to write a script, so it was a curious idea. The first thing in my odyssey was to go to Saskatoon for a special training course for travelling projectionists. I remember being extremely impressed by the possibility of this as a use of film.

It was quite new at the time and Grierson, realizing the great distances of the Canadian landscape and the distances between communities and so on, was going in for travelling projectors in a big way, but not only travelling projectors, not just a van taking films round and switching them on and off. He was training all his projectionists to be discussion leaders. They used to have seminars in which they spent a week or ten days being taught how to lead a discussion, and how to answer questions.

Towards the end of this training, I was seized with extreme pains, and the doctor said I'd got appendicitis. I got a lot of medical introductions to people in Winnipeg, took my appendix down there, and presented a letter to George Ferguson, who said, "How do you do?" I said, "How do you do? Do you happen to know of a good surgeon?" He replied, "Yes, the best surgeon in Winnipeg is Dr. Thorlaksen, and he's a great friend of mine."

So that was cleared up, my appendix was removed, and it is in the Winnipeg Hospital Museum because it was the biggest one they'd ever seen.

This stop in Winnipeg, which is still one of my most favourite places in the world, was really terribly important to me because of the tremendous kindness shown me by the editors and their wives of the two papers. George and Mary Ferguson of the *Free Press*, and John and Florence Bird of the *Tribune* couldn't have been kinder, nor could they have been more useful. They used to come in the evening, sit and talk, and they gave me a wonderful feeling of beginning to understand this enormous, beautiful, and underpopulated country.

I went down to Vancouver to recuperate, but couldn't go to Hollywood. Eventually I returned to the central area of Canada, and began interviewing hundreds of people in all walks of life about the importance of transportation in time of war, and Canada's relations with other countries, particularly the United States.

Finally I was brainwashed into feeling that I understood Canada, and that I could perhaps get some of this Canadian thinking into my craw. The interesting thing about all this is that I wasn't talking about films, and yet films were the trigger that set off the whole operation.

Eventually I received a curt note saying that I would be returning to England by boat, and should go to New York, where I found a representative of the British staff, a man called M. R. K. Burge. He wrote very good detective novels. He came over to me and said, "Look, the British government has arranged for the editors of all the principal Canadian newspapers to visit England. They will be given a personal interview with Winston Churchill, and they are going on the same transport as you. Could I make you a courier to ease their journey, and see that everything will be all right?"

I agreed. Well, it was the *Queen Mary* again, but under rather different circumstances, because she was a troop ship now. I was shoved onto this boat with these eminent editors, including George Ferguson and John Bird, and eight thousand other souls.

It was possible to serve only one meal a day, so you had to choose what hour of the day to have it. The ship ran into the worst storm the Atlantic had known for years. The ship took a terrible lurch and one of our members nearly went overboard. It was an absolutely miserable voyage and I thought to myself, "Well, never mind. We shall get to either Glasgow or Liverpool and the flags will be flying, I hope, particularly the one with the maple leaf on it, and all will be well."

When we got to Glasgow, I said to the assembled editors, "Now you all stand there. A boat will come in a minute to take you ashore, and then we'll take you to London." No boat came. There were no messages, and I realized that the British civil service was making as many mistakes as possible in the shortest possible time. So I said, "Well, never mind, they're probably waiting for you at the railway station," and I put them onto a filthy train that staggered along at about ten miles an hour into Glasgow.

I said to George Ferguson, "On my knees, I beg you, keep all your colleagues happy and cheerful because I don't know what's going to happen, and I've got to get on the telephone." Since it was Sunday, the offices were closed, and I couldn't even call Canada House.

Eventually I rang my parents, who knew the whereabouts of

another great figure in the history of documentary, J. P. R. Golightly, who also worked over here later during World War Two.
My parents kept saying, "How are you? Are you having a good
time?" I said, "Shut up. Now get hold of Golightly and, if you can't
get hold of him, do this yourselves. Get four large Daimler saloon
motor-cars and have them at Euston at ten in the evening." It was
already past noon, and I didn't really know if the message got
through.

The editors were getting a big edgy by now. It wasn't what
they'd expected, and there was absolutely no food or refreshments
on the train. I can only admit my relief that, when we pulled into
Euston many hours later, there were the four large Daimlers.

The gentleman from the foreign office came over and I said to
him, "What the hell happened?" He looked embarrassed and an-
swered, "Well, actually, owing to a slight departmental muddle, we
went to meet them at Liverpool, not Glasgow."

Back in England, I had to consider what to do next. Grierson
wanted a picture of Canada shown as Canada is, not as the British
thought it was. In another manifestation of my life, I had been film
critic for a London periodical called the *Spectator*. It was an influential liberal paper in the nice right-wing way of liberals, so I asked
the editor about it.

"Could I write some articles about Canada? I've just been there
for some time, and Grierson and I think there's a certain misun-
derstanding about what Canada is and what Canada is going to be.
If that could be cleared up, it might help the relations between the
two countries." He said, "Yes, do it, by all means," and I wrote two
articles.

I would like to read parts of these, which I think will be of
interest to you. Since I had been indoctrinated by Grierson, I was
representing his point of view as well as the point of view that I
remember the Canadian government having at that time. It can be
compared with what has happened in the interim, and what is
happening now. These articles were written in February, 1944.

CANADA AND THE WORLD

It is perhaps a commonplace to remark that the people of
Britain are, in general, remarkably ill-informed about their
fellow-members of the British Commonwealth. The rea-

sons for this ignorance are less important than the need for getting rid of it as soon as possible, and it is of special importance for us to get a clear conception of Canada's attitude towards the Commonwealth conception and towards world politics. Almost any Englishman who visits Canada (as I have just done) finds himself profoundly concerned with the need for a close and realistic understanding between the people of the two countries on these vital issues. The old romantic clichés of an outworn Imperialism are not only out of date, they are also dangerous.

Canada is acutely conscious of her status as a free nation. She is also acutely conscious of her geographical position in a world which is busy revising all its map-projections to meet new facts of global strategy. For today Canada lies exactly between two great world powers — the U.S.A. to the South and the U.S.S.R. to the North. Furthermore, it is across her territory that many of the main world air-routes lie. With her enormous natural resources and her rapidly multiplying industrial wealth well to the forefront of her national consciousness, Canada realises that her stake in a real world comity is as vital as that of any nation on the earth, and she is approaching the problem of her world position with considerable realism.

Some people may be shocked at the idea of stressing these somewhat brutal facts before any mention of "ties of blood and affection" and similar relationships. The answer is that there has been — on both sides — too much woolly sentimentalism and too little mutual understanding of the factual issues. It must be remembered, too, that of Canada's total population 30 per cent are French, 20 per cent German, Scandinavian, Ukrainian, Polish, Italian, Chinese and the like, and 50 per cent British — that is, Irish and Scots as well as English. In other words half the Canadian population has no roots in Britain and no *a priori* impulses of loyalty or duty towards her.

All are human beings, and all are *Canadians*.

All this is not to deny or decry the very real ties of friendship which exist. In this war the evidence is ever before our eyes. But it is urgently important for the British not to over-simplify the situation, and to assess it realistically. On the realistic basis the fact remains that neither country can do without the other. Even those few French-Canadians who demand outright secession will, if pressed, recognise that without the British link Canada as a nation would quickly be engulfed in the North American economy, and would retain independence in name only.

What, then, is Canada's conception of the role of the British Commonwealth in world affairs? In general, one may say that Canada's foreign policy is deeply concerned with a total internationalism, in which the Commonwealth can and must play a vital part. That is, she relates the Commonwealth idea to internationalism, rather than internationalism to the Commonwealth. In an address to the Foreign Trade Convention in New York last autumn, Brooke Claxton (Assistant to the Prime Minister of Canada) pointed out that "Canada has a vital interest in the growth of international trade on a multilateral basis.... Only multilateral trade and multilateral financial agreements can... enable us to use our export surplus to the United Kingdom and other countries to pay for our import surplus from the United States."

It must be realised that there are many Canadians who feel that Britain, in her Commonwealth relationships, has not shown all the progressiveness and enlightenment which she should have shown. They have not been over-favourably impressed either by Winston Churchill's *obiter dicta* on the future of the Empire, or by General Smuts's now famous speech, or, more recently, by the address given in Toronto by Lord Halifax, to which Mackenzie King replied in polite but unequivocally negative terms. This attitude, as was made plain, does not in any sense indicate a withdrawal from the Commonwealth conception, but a realistic approach to new developments of the Commonwealth idea — an approach which naturally reflects Canada's own sense of her present position and problems. It may be an indication of this realistic approach that one finds an increasing inhibition, in Ottawa and elsewhere, against the use of realistic approach to Commonwealth problems by the British Government will soon be overdue.

It may be worth while to take an actual situation and consider the possible divergencies of attitude which might arise therefrom. The question of the organisation of world

113

air-routes is a matter of deep discussion among the United Nations, and it is one in which Canada, by geographical position alone, is deeply implicated. Canada, on the functional basis of international organisation already mentioned, would expect full membership of any world body set up to deal with these matters; and the fact that many vital airfields are on Canadian territory naturally emphasises that claim. Now suppose that in the meantime Britain should propose the formation of a Commonwealth air-route scheme under the aegis, say, of a reconstituted B.O.A.C., and should further propose that this Commonwealth organisation should be the body which should negotiate in any international discussions on air-routes. One may justifiably guess that Canada would disagree with these proposals, and would urge that the matter should be approached from exactly the opposite angle. In other words, she would suggest a World Conference at which the Dominions, equally with any other nations vitally concerned, should be individually represented, and that *only in terms of reaching a world agreement on air transport* should the structure of the Commonwealth air-routes be discussed — if necessary, subsequent to the major decisions. If this hypothetical case seems over-simplified, it may be none the less valuable as an example of possibly basic divergences of opinion between the two countries which must at all costs be avoided.

In the end, Canada's stake in Britain is a stake in internationalism; and we in Britain would make a fundamental mistake if we were to underestimate the power and the value of the international thinking and planning which is to be found in Ottawa — notably in the departments concerned with finance, information and external affairs. We have as much to learn from Canada as Canada has from us.

CANADA AT HOME

Last week I discussed in *The Spectator* Canada's position in the world. Canada in herself, Canada at home, is a subject at least equally deserving of attention. For in this country we know Canada far too little. The limits of her natural resources cannot yet be accurately forecast. The vast mineral wealth of the Great Laurentian shield (that great arc of pre-Cambrian rock formation which is perhaps the most significant aspect of Canada's geological structure) has, in the opinion of some, hardly been scratched. On the other hand, the pioneer stage in agriculture has been passed; the Prairie Provinces have now recovered from the great drought of the 'thirties, which so tragically coincided with the world economic slump, and which revealed also that the dangers of erosion from over-exploitation of the soil were as present in Canada as in the dust-bowl further south. Conservation is now the watchword here (as, too, in the timber industry), and close study is being made of the possibility of alternative crops to wheat and also of the developments in the fascinating realm of chemurgy, since many prairie farmers feel that they dare not again risk putting all their eggs in one basket.

Developments in other fields have been dramatically rapid. Not only is Canada now the greatest base-metal exporter in the world; even more important is the fact that in the past few years her industrial expansion has been enormous. The main centres of industry tended originally to concentrate in Southern Ontario, an area which is economically much of a piece with the United States industrial areas around Buffalo, Detroit and Cleveland. The "metropolitan tug" of the U.S. centres, together with the strength of U.S. large-scale enterprise, has, as is well known, made it necessary to nurture Canadian industry by means of a pretty stiff tariff-barrier. Today Canadian industry is much nearer to a position in which it can stand on its own feet.

A further point regarding Canadian industry concerns Quebec, which is the second largest industrial area of Canada, but not the second wealthiest. Industrial expansion has hitherto been limited by the lower standards of living and, particularly, of technical education in this province. These lower standards have been both an indication of the French Canadian's individuality and at the same time one of the results of the Church's conscious attempt (in itself quite proper) to prevent the dissipation of the Catholic religion and of French culture under the impact of industrialism. As regards French-Canadian culture (using the word in its widest sense), it would appear that its disappearance would be a major disaster, since it represents a centuries-old thread of civilisation which is not only intrinsically valuable, but also is something which the rest of Canada — rawer and newer and only just out of the pioneering stage — tends to lack. As regards the other aspect, whether purely religious (clerico-paternalistic) or purely "nationalist" in the narrow sense, there are signs that the authorities of Quebec are changing their viewpoint to meet these changing times, and are giving at the least a qualified blessing to the institution of higher standards of technical and scientific education. The province has just passed its first Compulsory Education Act.

No review of Canada's potentialities can omit consideration of the future possibilities of those enormous territories which, almost overnight, have become an area of prime importance not only to Canada but also to all of the United Nations. The North-West Territories above latitude 60 degrees cover nearly one-third of Canada's land area. Known for years as an area of difficult transport in which the fur-trapper made his dangerous but profitable journeys, and as the land of the famous Yukon gold-rush, it was only after the last war that the development of the aeroplane began to forecast greater possibilities there. The pioneer efforts of the bush pilots, allied to the more scientific explorations initiated by the Canadian Government, revealed the existence of mineral deposits — notably oil — and of precious radium deposits in the pitch-blende around Great Bear Lake. Air transport over the North-West made considerable strides, and whole communities were served and supplied from the air. But it was not until the present war that military necessities compelled a real concentration on these territories. All the world knows of the great Alcan Highway, constructed at a cost and speed equally extraordinary; of the Canal Project, designed to unleash the oil wells of Norman; and of the construction of chains of airfields and landing-grounds which are the beginning of the transpolar air-routes which are now transforming all our conceptions of global strategy and travel.

But Canadian opinion is sharply divided as regards the future of the North-West. The enthusiasts claim that we are witnessing the conquest of Canada's last and most important frontier. They look to the discovery of more and more mineral deposits. They point out that climatic conditions are not so terrible as they have hitherto been assumed to be; at Aklavik, which is within the Arctic Circle, good vegetable crops can be grown during the short summer months, and further South there are at least two areas capable of limited but useful wheat production. The completed Alcan Highway will not only be a vital staging-route for the supply of the great air-bases, it will also resound to the cheerful klaxons of great hordes of automobile tourists from Canada and the United States; and both Alaska and the North-West will become summer playgrounds.

The other school of thought prefers to approach the North-West with a certain caution. It points out that the vast works now in progress stem from urgent military necessities, which are not necessarily the same as peace-time needs. The Alcan Highway is, therefore, more of a military undertaking by Canada and the U.S.A. than any-thing else. Will Canada, it is asked, be able to face the enormous upkeep cost of the highway under a peace-time economy? The sceptics further claim that there is as yet no certain knowledge of the make-up of mineral deposits in the North-West, and that too much confidence must not be placed in their inexhaustibility. The true answer will prob-ably be found to lie somewhere between these two extreme points of view. It seems certain that as regards long-distance flying the routes across the North-West Territories will remain vital, and will be much expanded.

In considering the future population of the North-West, the Eskimo race would appear to be of considerable impor-tance. The Eskimos, unlike the Indians, are not a dying race, and they show every sign of being able to assimilate some of the ideas and skills of modern Western civilisation. It seems likely that the Canadian Government, which has already shown a close interest in the development of the Eskimo, and which has already introduced reindeer to their territories to compensate for the dwindling of the caribou herds, will in the post-war period take further steps which will match the work being done by the U.S.S.R. authorities on the Northern Tundra of Russia.

When one views in all their vast perspective the resources of the whole of Canada, the question of population begins to assume major proportions. Nearly all Canadians would agree that 11½ million is a completely inadequate figure; that Canada could, on a conservative estimate, double her present population, and that in doing so she would increase her productivity and prosperity to a very great degree. Various estimates have been given of the total population which Canada could support under optimum conditions of world economic organisation. They range from 35 millions to 150 millions. The latter figure presumably refers to a distant future, when the populating of the Northern Tundra under reasonable living conditions becomes a practical possibility. For immediate purposes the figure of 35 million is probably the most sensible to consider. How this is to be achieved is a matter for argument. The Federal Government has not yet made any statement on a post-war immigration policy; but one may presume that it will not be much longer delayed. That a carefully planned and properly safeguarded policy of immigration is a matter of necessity for Canada would be denied by few. It would bring to more rapid fruition those great possibilities both for Canada and the world which are now so abundantly and vigorously evident.

In these articles, I do allude to the French situation because this was one of the things that Grierson particularly rubbed my nose in. Philéas Coté, who helped him, taught me as much about French Canada as anybody could. Of course, historically, some of it is now nonsense, but it's what Grierson was thinking, and he used me as a ventriloquist's dummy.

In closing, I want to say that this series of meetings has been an absolute revelation of what seems to me to be material of the highest standard, and I only wish my visit to Canada was not going to be so short. Thank you very much.

ROBERT ANDERSON

The NFB and the Private Sector

Panel discussion: Robert Anderson (moderator), Harry Gulkin, Judy Crawley, Gordon Sparling, Michael Spencer

Anderson: My name is Robert Anderson. Sam Kula couldn't come, so here am I, and Harry Gulkin, Gordon Sparling, Judy Crawley, and Mike Spencer. Julian Roffman was expected, but couldn't come.

So let me tell you how I first met Grierson. I was, at the time, program director of the CBC in Ottawa, and I found that all the excitement in town was centred around this strange place on John Street, in this crummy old building. There were people like Jimmy Beveridge coming up to rape the record library of the CBC to use as sound track in film music at the Film Board.

Gladstone Murray, then president of the CBC, said to me, "There's this very distinguished man from England, John Grierson, and I want you to put him on the air." So I arranged a series with Grierson. Well, this distinguished gentleman impressed the hell out of me. When he came to the studio, I assumed that, because of his experience, I wouldn't have to do anything to help him until he said, "Okay, you're a producer, produce me." So I did. Finally he said to me, "When are you going to stop fooling around here and come to work?"

Gladstone Murray loaned me to the Film Board for six months to work with Jimmy Beveridge and Boris Kauffman and Grant MacLean. We made a film on communications, shooting all over the country. After that, Grierson said, "It's not bad. You might as well stay around." I did, and I would echo Lou Applebaum when he said, "Grierson made me." The changes that man wrought in people were amazing, and today I'd go a country mile to make sure this university does something about a Grierson collection.

"Carleton University in Ottawa this week is also doing a seminar on Grierson. Does this signal a realization that Grierson was important? He was, to the nation and the world, enormously so. I couldn't speak to the Carleton students because I was coming here, so my wife and I were taped for the seminar. Our house was only a block away from the Film Board and, as everybody who worked at the Film Board knows, if there wasn't a crisis going on, Grierson would create one. One time I had to get Grierson out of the Film Board, so I took him over to my house. He talked to Catherine and cajoled her about being a housewife. Her answer to that was to write, in quick succession, ten plays for the CBC, which they bought and produced. While Grierson and Catherine were sitting and talking, Spottiswood went by on his bicycle, reading a script. He never wasted a moment of time. Grierson rapped on the window and Spottiswood ran into a telephone pole, which put Grierson in the greatest of humour.

I must tell you about my last meeting with Grierson. Just before he went to India, I heard he was giving a seminar at Carleton, so I went along. When he spotted me in the seminar, he said, "Do you know Bob Anderson? The Film Board's international reputation was largely made in its first years through Norman McLaren's films, and Bob Anderson's films about psychiatry."

Others here will have their own recollections of Grierson and, in deference to the lady present, we'll start with Judy Crawley, who was in on things from the beginning, and in the private sector.

Judith Crawley: Budge and I have always been in the private sector, although Grierson did invite us to join the Board. I would have done so, but Budge is very individualistic. It was certainly Grierson who put us on the road. If Marius Barbeau is the grandfather of Crawley Films, John Grierson certainly was the godfather.

I first met Grierson at the National Gallery. The director, Harry McCurrey, had just seen a little silent film we had made on L'Ile d'Orléans, near Quebec, and he asked John Grierson to come to the gallery and see the picture. He apparently thought that these two young people (the Crawleys) might be useful, and then Stuart Legg came along.

At that time, Budge was teaching me to do camera work. We were making a film on spring wild flowers. They, at least, would stay still while I focussed, and I could learn that way. Grierson said to Legg, "Come and look at this picture." It was called *A Study of Spring Wild Flowers*. I still remember his wonderful reaction, his slow smile and thoughtfulness. After the screen went dark, he put his hands up, looked at me, and said, "Strange new shapes." From then on, I thought I was in as a cameraman.

The next formal occasion, aside from various parties, Grierson called me one day and said, "Judy, can you cook?" I was a little stunned. I hadn't been married long, so I said "Why?" Grierson replied, "There's a surplus of apples in the Maritimes and I think, if we can promise them a film on cooking apples, we can get some money for the first colour motion picture made by the government." I said, "Of course I can cook," immediately rushed off to the Department of Agriculture, and got some recipes. We made the picture, and that was it.

From then on, we were free-lancing. Budge and I took turns as cameraman, and we did some editing. Grierson was wonderful, always lending us film and equipment. He'd say, "Come on, use the Film Board equipment at night." I remember, after our first baby, we'd take her in a basket every evening, go down to the Board, and use the thirty-five mm editing equipment. In the morning, when the char-ladies came, we would pick up the baby and leave. We used to meet the film Board people coming in. All I'd like to say is, like Lou and Bob, Crawley Films would never have existed if it hadn't been for Grierson.

Anderson: Gordon Sparling is the senior here. He knew him before many of us did.

Gordon Sparling: When I first met Grierson, there wasn't much of a private sector. There was one large firm and one or two little one-man operations. Associated Screen was a big established outfit with about two hundred employees and, unfortunately, Grierson's opening remark to some reporters was taken out of context. The reporters asked him, "What are you going to do over here?" He replied, "I'm going to start a film industry," meaning within the government. His idea was a governmental film board, but it wasn't reported accurately. The president of our firm was a stodgy little fellow and he didn't like the remark. As Grierson got more active, of course, his work was cutting into the revenues of Associated. The Post Office Department, for instance, made a Christmas trailer every year, *Why Grandma's Parcel Was Late*. When Grierson passed the act that said all work had to be handled by the government, the president, Mr. Norwitch, was furious. Grierson had a job to do. He was starting a Film Board, but he had no equipment or experienced people, so he relied on us for the work.

The early recordings were done at our studio, including the Voice of Doom.

Anderson: Lorne Greene was an announcer on the CBC staff when I was program director.

Sparling: I remember the music for McLaren's *Dollar Dance* being done. "Canada Carries On" was recorded in our place for the first couple of years. There was a kind of rivalry. What I mean is, the private sector versus the government created a slight tenseness. Grierson used to phone and say, "Can you come up to Ottawa? I've got an idea." We'd go, and he'd describe this wonderful picture he had in mind with lots of glowing details, and we'd leave thinking, "This is going to be the picture to end all pictures." Halfway back from Ottawa, I'd think, "What the hell did he say anyway?" We did quite a few pictures for the Board; the biggest one was *Peoples of Canada*. Ross Beasley and I travelled across Canada in eight weeks, and made a three-reel epic.

The last time I saw Grierson was on the occasion of the twenty-fifth anniversary. I heard a voice from the other side of the crowded stage at the Film Board — "There's my friendly enemy" — and he came roaring across. We shook hands and had a nice reunion.

Anderson: Mike Spencer was among the first at the Film Board.

Michael Spencer: I was going to talk about how I came to work at the National Film Board. I was in New York in the fall of 1939, just after the war started. I'd been a member of the Oxford Film Society, knew a lot about documentary, but don't remember how I discovered that Grierson was in Canada. It seemed surprising to me, but I left New York immediately on a bus, came to Ottawa, and asked him for a job. According to most of the people who have talked so far, Grierson was after them. In my case, I was trying to get a job with Grierson; I wanted to work for the National Film Board. I wanted to make movies.

In New York, I had made a small sixteen-mm silent, black-and-white film. When I went to see Grierson, I had some still photographs, and my little movie. He wasn't terribly interested in the film, or in the stills, and I got the impression that I was wasting my time. At the end of the conversation, however, he said, "You'd better take that film down and show it to Stuart Legg." After looking at it, Legg said, "Well, I guess you know what you're doing. I think perhaps we can use you."

Next day I returned to Grierson's office for the final verdict. Grierson was engaged in a fight with Frank Badgley, who was running the Canadian government Motion Picture Bureau. Over the phone, Grierson said to Badgley, "I want you to take this guy Spencer," and Badgley's reply was, "I'm not taking any more of those young punks. Do something else with him."

So my first job was working for Crawley Films. They had an assignment to do a film called *Iceland on the Prairies*. I was to be general assistant on all aspects of the picture. That's how I met Margaret Ann, and the late Graham McInnis, who were both there in Winnipeg making this film. My relationship with Grierson had ceased because I was working for the Crawleys.

On Saturday nights there was usually a traditional party going on at John Street. Grierson showed up there from time to time. A year later, in August 1941, when I was a private in the army, I went along to one of these parties. Grierson asked me what I was doing. I told him, and he said, "I've got plans for you, Spencer. We're going to have a big army and navy unit, and you're going to be the captain in charge." That made me very excited, so I did my military training, and dreamed about being the guy in charge of all the National Defence film operations. In August, I was asked if I would go on active service, so I said yes immediately. Within three or four days, I was on a boat going to England. I had my own documents, something unheard of for a private to travel with his own documents.

On the second day out, I met Grierson who said, "I'm on my way over to London, to set this whole thing up for you." I thought, "Here we go again." He had a thirty-five-mm Neimo camera with a couple of thousand feet of film. I was suddenly hauled up and was told to stay on the bridge all the time because Grierson thought that this troop ship would probably be torpedoed, so it was important to take some pictures of it. I went all across the Atlantic in about eight days and the only thing that happened was that, one day, one of the ships began to zigzag. They used to go one way for thirty minutes, and then the other way for another thirty minutes. I noticed that the ship on the right seemed to be getting very close to us. No one seemed to be paying any attention. So I went to a guy on the bridge and asked him, "Is that right?" and he said, "Gawd!" The other ship managed to veer away, so we were all right, and we weren't torpedoed. I spent the next six weeks in London with Grierson as his executive assistant. I was drafting letters, going to screenings, everything. Grierson was at the top of his form. He was trying to take over the whole operation of the Defence Film Unit, and he was using the film act, which gave him the power that brought him suspension. The army said, "That's the national film act; when we're over here, we do our own thing. Thank you." Jack Macdougall and myself and a couple of other guys finished up in the Army Film Unit. Later on, Gordon joined us. From then on, Grierson didn't have anything to do with the Canadian Army Film Unit. We heard no more about him until 1944 when he came back for three days, and spent two days with the guys on the front lines who were shooting pictures. Julian Roffman was there too.

Anderson: Now here's Harry Gulkin who's only been involved for about twelve years. He's a feature-film producer, has made *Lies My Father Told Me* and *Two Solitudes*. He comes from a commercial background, a real film producer. The private sector.

Harry Gulkin: In 1968 a friend, Marilee Pascal, said, "Grierson's back in Montreal, and he's giving a course at McGill. Come on down." So I came as an uninvited, over-ripe, mature student and went to the first session. Grierson looked around and said, "If there is anyone here who is uninvited, would they please announce themselves?" A young woman sitting in the corner put up her hand timorously. He said, "Oh, no, not you, dear," and dropped the subject.

I remember that the course wasn't at all what I'd expected. The first day he began to talk about space and its meaning to Canadians. He began creating a definition, a series of perceptions towards the students, of what being Canadian was about. Slowly he began to build around that during the thirteen weeks and I came away with a sense of rootedness, not locality but of nation. He described it with great eloquence. Adam Semansky, Ron Blumer and Marilee Pascal were all there. A large proportion of film students have found their way into active positions, directing, producing, writing, and editing in this country's film industry. Some things that struck me as important were, "People with eight-mm minds shouldn't make thirty-five-mm films," and "The eight-mm camera is the ball-point pen of the 1970s looking ahead to the next decade."

I did get to know Grierson a bit, but I think he thought rather more of my knowledge and background than was realistic. He asked me to arrange a meeting for him with some of the people in the private sector. I knew a few, and I arranged a small meeting at his Crescent Street hotel. We talked, and he expressed a real interest in my ideas, and advised me on an irregular basis over the next few months. He permitted me to name him as a member of a non-existent advisory committee to my newly formed film company, and it was announced in *The Gazette*. Then he said, "The guy we've got to get is Spencer because he's sitting on all the money." Spencer was head of CFDC. We had lunch but he wasn't impressed. We had to attend many other activities before we could get anywhere, and things didn't work out for a couple of years. A few years later, when I ran into Grierson, I told him I was making the film, and his response was, "But it took so long, Harry, so long," and it does.

Anderson: Did you notice? Grierson called Spencer "Spencer." Nobody ever called Grierson "John" or "Mr. Grierson." He was always "Grierson." I wonder if Grierson would have gone on, as the Film Board did, to do anything questionable, immoral, or wrong; for example, barring independent production companies from making films for government departments without Film Board supervision. I believe that you cannot work for two masters and, certainly, there were periods when the Film Board was permitting people in the private sector, who wanted to make films for government departments, to see only a limited number of people. Ideas had to be vetted with the Film Board, and the Film Board would decide whether a film should be made or not. I never made a film for the Film Board after I left in 1955 to start my own company, the principal reason being that I didn't want to be told how to make my film. It's a point of contention, and I wonder whether Grierson would have approved. The film act has been greatly misused. It's a weak instrument, and could have been broken at any time. The Film Board, however, is too valuable an institution to destroy.

Kirwan Cox (from the audience): As for Grierson's attitude towards film, we must go back to 1938, when he came to Canada to report on the status of film-making in the country. He was very specific and said that, since there was no central film-making organization in the country with a government-sponsored program, one was needed. Otherwise, there would be a lot of waste and duplication, and it would lead to a lot of bad movies being made. Since there were experts in various government departments, for example, the hydro-power group or the agriculturalists, they could be called on for advice, but since they knew nothing about making films, Grierson felt that government film-making should be sponsored to ensure quality film-making. The combination, according to Grierson, of expertise in the field and in the film-making would "bring the issue alive."

Anderson: Kirwan, you're talking about a different period of time.
Robert Verrall: (from the audience): I got to know Grierson once he came to McGill. He was very concerned that the Film Board not abdicate its duties towards the departments, and he was concerned about what he perceived to be a growing attitude among the Film Board film-makers. Grierson saw the Board as having an important rôle in the future of the film program with the departments, but not exclusively. The job to be done was bigger than could be done by only one agency.
Anderson: I'm not talking about not being involved, but about an open, competitive situation.
Liz Avison (from the audience): I wonder if something can be done about the lack of a distribution system. We should really make more of Grierson's films accessible. I agree that the national film act is still an unsolved problem, and that it's an important one to tackle. The Film Board may have a mechanism to assist with that.
Anderson: I wish we could recreate the kind of distribution as suggested by Jim Beveridge, the kind of thing that was going on in the Film Board in the early years, when distribution was taken rurally. A lot of film courses are being conducted in this country. When I'm asked to speak to university classes, the first thing I say is, "How many of you people have made a film?" At least forty percent hold up their hands, and I wonder about these kids going through these film schools. What are we going to do with them? Companies like mine, with small staffs, can't take them on. We should be sharing our experiences with these young kids. They're probably imbued with the kind of thing that we got drunk on years ago. They're attending schools directed by people who have largely come out of the Griersonian tradition. I wonder if we can't generate something of the kind that Jimmy [Beveridge] wanted to see happen. The problem is there isn't any work.
Gulkin: Jim Beveridge described the distribution network last night, and it was extraordinary, that pre-television network. The requirements for such a travelling network, however, are no longer there. The level of television penetration is so great in the country, it really is a question of film-makers having access in the first place. Films are designed primarily for theatrical release to the television-market outlet, so it's more difficult for design. A series of grass-roots elements no longer exists. People don't go to church basements to watch movies anymore to any degree. They have a television set. Most cultural events that can go onto film or video-

tape should be designed for television, and that creates a problem. There are few buyers. On the other hand, a vast market in distribution does exist.

Elspeth Chisholm: I'd just like to say that private films are far too expensive for colleges to afford in their budgets, so I used NFB films, not only because I like them and I like what they do, but because the private films are too expensive to rent. *Bethune* was probably no more than an hour, because otherwise I wouldn't have used it. Your class wouldn't last more than an hour.

Anderson: Where the Film Board and the CBC have failed over the years is not to reach some rapprochement that would lead to sensible use of NFB films. I remember Davidson Dunton and Arthur Irwin and I sitting on the dock in front of our cottage talking about how to get the Film Board and the CBC together; how to make some kind of working arrangement. That was in 1950. It has never been achieved. In 1967 there was to be a survey of films for Centennial Year. My company was retained to do it. I reported to Judy Lamarsh, the Secretary of State. The CBC wouldn't even admit they made films; that was the Film Board's job. Al Ouimet, the president, had set up a committee to deal with me. No, they didn't make films. I said unless I had the information by the next day I would go back to Al; if I didn't get it from him, I'd go to Judy; if I didn't get it from her, I'd have it raised in Parliament. The next day it turned out that they had made some 400 films the past year. That was far more than the Film Board had made. I went to Roberge, head of the Film Board. He absolutely refused information; they were *his* films. It happened that day I was having lunch with Miss Lamarsh. We had drinks and took our time getting back to her office, although she said someone was waiting to see her. It turned out it was Roberge. I got the information I needed. All this was published in our report and we were very critical of both agencies. The Film Board has not forgiven us.

Susan Schouten-Levine (from the audience): Film distribution is difficult. I saw a film on television one time, and I wanted to see it again, but there was simply no way of getting it. Now there is some distribution of films, at least. It costs too much money to buy the rights. Some are not available. The private sector has difficulty in the education section because of cost. Private markets have to make a decent return on their investment to stay in the business; therefore, they have to charge a substantial rental fee. So educational institutions, which should be a major market, can't participate. Their budgets are being constantly cut back. It's a vicious circle.

Anderson: If we are dealing with the private sector, we must realize that a critical criterion for them is to at least return the cost of the film-making. If the films cannot be sold to theatres or existing distribution networks, where is the money going to come from to make these films? Only one distribution system generates dollars, and that is advertising, fundamentally. Regrettably, it has a degrading effect. If there is a battle, it is in turning the distribution arena into one where material is distributed that is good, decent, experimental, and innovative. It should stimulate film-makers in the private sector. If they get paid, we'll find a market for it.

Crawley: For about fifteen years of my life, I was able to keep a fair-sized section of Crawley Films operating on educational films but, during those fifteen years, there was not one school film that was financed in Canada. I had to go to the American market — McGraw-Hill, Encyclopaedia Britannica. In California, I could recover money from one source. When a country has ten provinces, each with its own educational system, and no single source to approach, the only way was to go to the American market. That is a sad commentary on Canada. When I got into producing, industrial films were definitely slanted. If somebody's putting up fifty thousand dollars, he has something he wants to say, and it's the film-maker's responsibility to make it say something useful. I succeeded often. The toughest was when the Exxon Corporation came from New York and said, "We would like a film on conservation." I said, "Impossible," but in the end, we produced it. We produced a film for the United Nations, too. It can be done, especially if you've been inspired in your youth by Grierson. With proper incentives and patience, you can sometimes turn the sponsor around, but you still don't have any network. It's a case of each individual film or series.

During the war years, sixteen-mm film was rationed. Unless you were doing something for the government, for Grierson, you couldn't have any film. Grierson had no objection to the private sector being encouraged. He always encouraged us. He gave us recruiting films. I spent months moving little Dinky-Toy tanks around, and making tank-training films. He used the private sector for producing. There must have been five companies. There was no industry at that time, and Grierson employed all the country's film skills to do what he thought were useful things, and he continued to do so.

The day Grierson left, an unfortunate wave of paranoia swept through. It was around the time of the political problems, and somehow that reflected on the almost non-existent private sector. The other day, for instance, I heard an unbelievable story — Budge Crawley was supposed to have written a letter to poison some government people against John Grierson. Of course, it's untrue. It was a result of the paranoia on the part of certain people at the Film Board, and it happened just after Grierson had gone. When Grierson left, Budge and Roby Kidd wrote, telephoned, or personally addressed twelve universities in Canada, including this one, to ask them to give John Grierson an honourary degree. Not one would endorse it. The paranoia was there, and it didn't spring only from private industry.

Anderson: When I was on leave in New York in 1949, I had a board of distinguished psychiatrists who were involved with a lot of United States money for mental-health films. When the would-be producers came, I said could I see something they had made. Nine out of ten said "here is the film, but you must remember, it's what the sponsor wanted". That simply means they had given up their responsibility as film makers. Later, when I proposed to my board that certain producers do certain subjects, they were called communists suddenly by a producer who wanted to corner the work for himself. Some of this paranoia is still going on.

When Grierson moved to the States and confronted this documentary community, the great white saviours, the so-called fathers of documentary in the United States, they involved him in this witch-hunt atmosphere, too. They didn't want the competition.

I had lunch this week with six former ambassadors, including Charles Ritchie, Charles Woodsworth, who supported the Film Board when he was editor of the *Citizen*, John Starnes, former head of RCMP security, and Mark McClung, also in security. Mark said, "In all the RCMP files about Grierson, there was not one single thing said to implicate him, except through Freda Linton. She was his secretary. Nevertheless, there was nothing to tar his name.

Crawley: There was an attempt at good-will on both sides, and that's a personal feeling because I've never felt any animosity.

Spencer: The private sector has been feeling its oats in the last few years, and that's because it's been doing a lot of good work. It's trying to challenge the Film Board at various levels, and that's good.

When I returned to the Board in 1946, the staff had a strong anti-private-sector bias. Never, while I was there, however, was there any serious discussion about giving any money to anyone in the private sector. For twenty-five years, the private sector has had meetings with the CBC, but their ideas are usually rejected. The CBC continues to produce the film material.

The private sector now has enough people to do something significant. It obviously wants to be taken seriously in terms of making central films to interpret Canadians.

Colin Low (from the audience): There are enormous problems, and equitable distribution is only one. Because I'm from the west, I've been interested in how to get around the problems. For a long time, the people in the Film Board have had an understanding of this lack of equity, and the attempt to be decentralized. In the early 1970s, there was some transferral of staff so that a small production nucleus in each major area could be formed. Now it's been given over to the regional people; they've hired other regional people on a free-lance basis. Small companies have been given a chance and some of the best things done this year are private-sector films. When I hear that the Film Board has been antipathetic and selfish, I find I can't buy it.

Crawley: I think you're talking about the last ten years, Colin, but there was a period when those who weren't in the Film Board had to go outside of the country for private funds, and you know that commercial films are not ideal work.

Spencer: I have just sat through three weeks of pay-TV hearings. Unfortunately, I didn't hear the Film Board's presentation because, instead of being broadcast on cable, it came on too late.

Robert Verrall: The only reason this industry can survive is because we have a lot of producers. We need more Judy Crawleys, but I don't know whether the system of regional production is creating producers. It's uncovering talent; maybe the next step would be the development of producers. You have to allow and encourage talent to arise.

Gulkin: So there's been some failure, but there are increasing efforts now, certainly by the Board. Two collaborators in the private sector have defined mechanisms by which they can work together, and I think there has been a genuine effort in that respect. In my personal experience in the last years, I think there has been a failure on the Board's part and the CBC's part. They are two mature, well-funded production organizations in the country and, in Canada, the private sector means something different than from most countries in the world.

There was no private sector in feature-film-making in this country until Mr. Spencer and his Canadian Film Development Corporation came on the scene about twelve years ago. There wasn't money for feature films until the Treasury Department, urged by the CFDC and various political lobbying groups, introduced something called the capital-cost allowance, which put taxpayers' money into an entreprenurial western private sector, which has gone out and found monies with a return for the investors, so they could make more movies.

These individuals with entreprenurial capabilities who exist outside larger organisms generate a great deal of activity, but only with the help of the public sector. That's a Canadian tradition. When the guys who started building the Lachine Canal ran out of money, the government bailed them out. And there's the St. Lawrence Seaway. When John A. MacDonald had to finish the CPR in 1885 because Riel was getting out of hand, we set up a public railroad to keep the CPR straight. The same goes for our telegraph system, our airlines, and communications. So, the fantasy of private entrepreneurs being somehow destroyed by governmental institutions is false, I think.

National Film Board films are noted for their form and content, their meaning, their relevant social content and some experimentation. Nothing has been less characteristic of the four hundred million dollars worth of films that have been made in the feature-film industry in the course of the last three or four years. Where we became experts in creating deals, incentives we had from raising monies brought the flow of private industry, who were less concerned with the process of making films beyond their potential return. So we had an influx of competent lawyers and accountants; we spent two hundred and fifty thousand dollars setting up a deal.

If any of the feature films began to look half as good as the beautiful four-colour investment prospectuses, we'd take over the world. I think the rôle of the Board and the CBC is to keep things straight. There is a point of contact that has relevance for Canadian audiences, to the extent that they relate to them. I think there are weaknesses, but we are fortunate in having, as a custodian, a conscience of film-making in the Griersonian tradition, and an organism that has become a national pride.

The National Film Board is recognized more outside the country than within, and I think we tend to go overboard when we hit at the warts. Problems of bureaucracy are inevitable in any forty-year-old organization. They must be dealt with, but I think the Board and the CBC will work things out and become partners with individual private producers. As examples, there's a very significant film, *Les Plouffes*, and there is the recent partnership with the Film Board and *Les Beaux Souvenirs*.

It is difficult, Mr. Spencer, for a private, individual producer to talk to eight people on the Board about the same subject. I had that problem trying to talk to you, to your attorney, to your budget guide, and all the others, and still have time to make a movie.

Spencer: May I ask a question here? Do you think the CFDC has any rôle to play in regard to the conscience?

Gulkin: I think it has; it is a critical component of the CFDC. If a government agency is putting money into movies, it has two objectives: quality and content. It has a responsibility to private investors, but its basic rôle is a fundamental watch-dog.

Spencer: It's important to realize that the CFDC is basically a spin-off from the National Film Board. It was created within the organization, with a certain amount of bad-tempered discussion. The Board felt that, under its act in 1964-65, it could undertake to produce feature films as well. The matter was discussed, and it was decided that it would be better to create another agency, in collaboration with the private sector. I think the CFDC, as a government agency, has a conscience rôle and, if the government is supporting the private sector in film, it should do it through the CFDC, which is primarily dedicated to the idea of developing and helping the private sector to produce, even though it is not a co-producer.

Tom Daly (from the audience): In my experience, the conscience has to lie with the film-maker, not with some agency trying to stop the film-maker. I had an interesting experience with NATO films. Each country made a film about its own country for all the other NATO countries. I tried not to get involved but, in the end, had to go to Paris. Several films were being shown, and the last one was an American one. The fellow in charge was so embarrassed (it was a private-sector film) that he asked me if I would look at it and see what could be done. The United States government had farmed the film out to *News of the Day*. They looked in their stock-pile library quickly, took a sequence from New England, other sequences from here and there, ran the same music over it, and added new commentary.

The point I'm making is that it was impossible to get them to rework it for United States national interest, so it's foolish to suggest that an organization will be the conscience and watch-dog of the content.

As for the Board, remember that responsibilities can gradually disappear over a generation, and maybe you think that this has happened at the NFB. I think it's possible for it to disappear in the private sector. For instance, there could never have been an NFB in the United States, even with Grierson, because the private sector already had made it an impossibility. Government-information-made films in the United States are based on making money, and films made by the United States government for use abroad have not been seen or checked by the American public. Other countries know them only as propaganda. The only exception was the Kennedy film. It was shown in the United States, but they had to pass an act of Congress in order to show it at home.

Grierson had a tradition, and he left it at the Film Board. There are two kinds of film needs, and I regret that, throughout the history, almost all the effort goes into the violence and very little into the other side. The Film Board has difficulty today finding sufficient finances for what they used to be able to do easily. The staff used to have enough program money to make use of all the private people. Now, the demand is enormous. For instance, it used to be hard to find even four summer students who were good and wanted to come to work. Later on, we received three hundred applications for six possible places; therefore, only six people in the private sector were satisfied and two hundred ninety-four were mad. There's no solution with that attitude.

Crawley: But there were another thousand out there who had been working in the industry, and had been hoping to get some work from the government, and they were mad, too.

Daly: Well, the only solution is for both sides to work together. We have had just as much difficulty with the CBC.

Spencer: Judy said the government, not the Film Board.

Crawley: I was talking about government work, not Film Board contracts.

Daly: There are other government departments, like the Swedish

133

Institute, where they simply cannot find people with the national kind of tradition, such as we have.

Cox: This is really not a significant issue, any more than it was an attempt thirty or forty years ago. You're talking hundreds of millions of dollars. Millions are being wasted, mismanaged, embarrassingly mismanaged, you know. The money spent for the private sector, to private ad agencies, has been well-spent. We get our patrons, and then we worry about the money that is misspent.

Crawley: Kirwan, you weren't there in the years when the angst was going on, and we were all trying to keep our heads above water.

Low: In this whole thing, though, the concern I have is in preserving this unique Griersonian tradition. How do you preserve it outside of the Film Board?

Spencer: Or even within the Film Board.

Low: Exactly. That is the major difficulty. When we started the regional program, there was a lot of resistance to the idea from the private sector, because they thought we were going to bring our staff and take away what little there was there. The criticism within the Film Board was leaving the film work to get more money for the private sector outside of the Grierson tradition.

It should be the leading concern of this group to preserve the survival of something that is unique in the world.

Crawley: I learned from my own experience in the United States that there's a tremendous respect for Canadian film-makers, and it all springs from the early Griersonian tradition, which is still carried on among a lot of the students and young people outside the Board today.

Gulkin: Let's talk about the Film Board and the CBC. We should have concern for the material, social resonance, and content, which people can relate to but which expresses docu-dramatic form almost exclusively. There have been some exciting innovations in drama and in the development of theatre, regional theatre particularly, in this country. Script writers reflect a rootedness but a great deal of experimentation, too, a nuance, and the development of a new aesthetic platform. Religious adulation of the documentary form as it travels into dramatic film is a very different kind of thing. What is not present at the Board or in the private sector is the kind of symbiotic relationship with theatre that has been characteristic of Warner Street for many years, and of every film centre in the world where there has been a cross-over between theatre and film, enabling film to reflect the state of the art as it has developed in theatre. If we maintain a purity of form as distinct from content, we will doom ourselves to a certain aridity of expression that will not find an audience. We really have to look outward in that, bearing in mind that our content must have some relevance.

Michael, you can speak to us much more effectively about the early wave of films in the seventies, feature films that were well-intentioned but equally bad. They didn't work. They told stories, but there was no knowledge of what a narrative curve is in terms of drama. Both directors and actors lacked experience. Documentary is more pure expression of the film-makers.

David Balkan (from the audience): What you're talking about at the moment includes the private sector in the United States and Great Britain. The CBC has not caught on yet to the mainstream and cultural changes. They never show contemporary dance and very seldom show any regional theatre. We must develop script writers through other media, and the transition of television is very important. We have a very rich private sector in broadcasting in Canada that has contributed next to nothing to our cultural development. Mr. Rice in Edmonton has built a wonderful theatre, but he never thinks of doing a play for the CBC network. The young people have to look somewhere for their learning opportunities. We've got thousands of people coming out of film schools. Where are we going to employ them all? They're not getting into television and they're not getting any experience. The Film Board's regional studios bring some of these people in, but it's a different private sector than we've been talking about. The question is, once they've gained their experience, where do they go?

Spencer: Pay-television is coming quickly and the markets are proliferating, and the amounts of money that have been promised by those people who've applied for licences is enormous.

Anderson: Peter Ohlin asked for an hour, and he's had far more than that.

PETER HARCOURT

Some Relationships Between the NFB Animation Department and the Documentary

Panel discussion: Peter Harcourt (moderator), Tom Daly, Colin Low, Gerald Potterton, Bob Verrall

Peter Harcourt: On the one occasion when I met the great John Grierson, I made the tactical error of introducing myself to him by declaring my institutional credentials. I told him that I had worked for a number of years at the British Film Institute, whereupon he launched into a twenty-two minute attack against everything that was wrong with it, explaining to me the many ways in which it had betrayed the essence of British film culture. That one meeting with John Grierson I'll always remember, although I'm sure he forgot it immediately. However, since I've been invited to chair this panel, I do want to say that I'm very pleased to be here at McGill's gathering of the clan of the house that Grierson built.

I should perhaps begin with a bit about my background. I lived for about fourteen years in Great Britain; and when I was working for the Film Institute, one of my jobs was to certify short films as "educational" so that they could be imported without duty into the country. This included, of course, films made by the National Film Board of Canada. That's where I got to see films like *City of Gold, I Was a Ninety-Pound Weakling, Lonely Boy*, and *Universe*. Names like Tom Daly, Roman Kroiter, Wolf Koenig, and Colin Low kept coming up in the credits. I'd been in England for over ten years by then and had become accustomed to thinking of myself as a North American. Seeing these films, however, from the NFB, made me say to myself: "These are not American films. These are not English films. These are Canadian films." I wanted to come home. Through seeing certain images — not necessarily of archetypal Canadian people (Paul Anka, God help us!) — but images that reflected a Canadian way of thinking, I began to rediscover, while working in England, my Canadian self. These films made me feel more Canadian, and I think this could be true for other people as well. When Canadians see pictures of themselves on Canadian screens, it helps us to know who we are. In any case, that's how it was with me. That's my story.

When I was invited to chair this discussion, I began to think about the influence of documentary on animation and of animation on documentary, for that is the topic of this panel. I'm still thinking about these influences and still without much clarity. But the Film Board has been a very privileged institution. Especially in the early days, people were able to move about among different divisions of work. They weren't labelled camera people and then stuck in a camera person's job or union. They weren't labelled editors and locked away in an editing box. In the early days, the Board was like a film school: people got to do everything. You could even learn to be a producer if you stayed there long enough! But everybody was exploring different kinds of experience. Some were dealing with the real world in the Griersonian sense of going out and capturing external reality on film; others — Norman McLaren, for example — were more concerned with a more interior reality, working in animation or writing directly on film. But all the people at this conference have worked both with documentary and with animated films. Wolf Koenig should be here because, not only has he spent many years in the animation studio but he is also one of Canada's finest documentary cinematographers.

Animation, then, might be said to represent the more introspective aspect of filmmaking. It can be done by a man alone in a room with an idea — like Norman McLaren with his flip books or whatever techniques he was investigating, creating from his personal imagination directly onto film. Documentary, on the other hand, is always altered by the reality it encounters. One has to go out and get it. But perhaps the fact that so many people at the Film Board have worked both in animation and in documentary explains to a degree the moral seriousness and introspective quality of so many Canadian documentary films. Take the films made in the '50s and '60s by Tom Daly's Unit B for example. Think of the introspective seriousness of even a comparatively silly film like *I Was a Ninety-Pound Weakling*, of the reflective quality in this film that questions the nature of the world. Maybe it was because people at the Board could go out and grab the real stuff of documentary and then retire to the animation studio to think about different things that helped to give their documentaries a more introspective quality. I don't know. This is just a hypothesis. This is what we might discuss.

Tom Daly: One day I asked Norman McLaren what this Grierson thing did to him when he was starting a new film. I didn't expect him to answer, really. Usually people say, "Oh, there are no words for that." But he said that he accepts a set of limitations, and further explained that the minute you started thinking about it, every single thought associated with a hundred others, and about two or three steps beyond, that he was totally out of his depth and totally confused. He set a definite, rigid set of limitations, and invented story elements within the rules of those limitations. For instance, *Spheres* — he set the limitations that everything would move at a regular pace, not the way it does in life but, if it went around a corner, it still went round the corner at the same pace as if it went straight, and all the movements are related to that. It's evident that the events that could happen in that world are quite different from those that might happen in a normal world. He didn't quite translate something from the normal world into another dress with the same script; he actually experimented to see what kind of events did happen in the other world. There's a little film called *Two Bagatelles*, which is part of that experimentation. He bound himself by the rules of the truth of the world he invented, just as rigidly as you were commenting that, in actuality, people are bound by the same rules. There's not all that much difference between the two, after all.

Peter Harcourt: Now, maybe there's another way of extending what you just said, Tom. The discipline involved in animation, as you described it through Norman's work, can be seen in the highly disciplined and formal work of Unit B also. Let's just leave that for a moment. I want to introduce the panel.

On my extreme left is Bob Verrall. He has worked in animation and has also produced live action films at the NFB. Colin Low is a fine film-maker and a producer in both animation and live action films. He's a great story-teller, too, as we know from yesterday. On my right is Gerald Potterton, who has worked in live action and animation both inside and outside the Board.

Gerald Potterton: I worked there thirteen years.

Peter Harcourt: I thought I'd ask each of you people to make a statement about your work and how it has differed inside and outside the animation field and in live action, whether in the documentary or fiction.

Bob Verrall: I don't remember sensing a division between the work of the animation studio and whatever else was going on at the Film Board. There was never an animation ghetto. When I arrived, my job was to do animated maps. That was one of the big jobs at the animation studio. I worked with Evelyn Lambert on some of the films that were being produced in "World in Action" and the "Canada Carries On" series. I didn't feel remote from the stars in the place. You were expected to show up at staff screenings of the latest documentary films. Sometimes your opinion was asked — whether you'd ever held a camera before or not. There was something about the nature of the organization that encouraged interchange between people working within animation and with people working within live action. So there was no hurdle to get over.

Peter Harcourt: Colin?

Colin Low: I think Bob has put his finger on it. When I arrived, about the same time, 1945, every live-action film had a map in it, partly because of the international series. Evelyn Lambert, working at Norman's elbow, was my teacher, and Bob's teacher and, for a long time, I thought that animation was maps. I did maps for army films and it left me with an impression of lines crawling across northern Canada — Exercise Lemming, Exercise Eskimo, Exercise Muskox, all army exercises and titles in the tundra. The first job I had was doing a title for Stuart Legg. It was *Food, Secret of the Peace*. I remember being sent in to Stuart Legg to see what he wanted, and he said, "I want a warehouse, absolutely crammed with barrels and boxes and what have you. It has to sort of diminish to infinity, and I want "FOOD" to come out of the back of this warehouse from infinity, and then come up, fade, and then come up again with "FOOD, SECRET OF THE PEACE." So I went away, got a big piece of cardboard, and started to draw this warehouse. Then, when I thought I had it, I would take it into Stuart Legg. he would say, "Not enough stuff. You haven't got enough." So I'd go back and rework this drawing, and take it back in about a week and a half (the cardboard was about that thick) and finally he said, "Okay, that's it." So for years we were continually in contact with people who were doing live-action films. We did sing-songs. Grierson said, "We've got to have some leavening to this program," so the leavening was the sing-song, bouncing balls, sing-alongs. For a long period of time, we made bouncing-ball films. Once I was in a theatre where I actually saw people sing along with one of our bouncing-ball films. Then finally, in the animation department, we acquired, with great luck, Tom Daly. He had a real interest in the graphic image, and used it with great effect before anybody else — *Hungry Minds* and *Kathy Kollowitz*. They were pictures in which some of the first graphic images were used brilliantly and integrated into the story. Tom became our producer and, inadvertantly, part of Unit B. We had a lot of luck, the acquisiton of people like Wolf, who came as a passionate camera nut and an inspired amateur cartoonist. He was a kid off a southern Ontario farm who was packed with talent, ambition, and energy. His job at the Film Board was splicing. Next thing we knew, Wolf Koenig was doing cartoons in the animation department, and editing people's films in the splicing room. Animation is a very exciting field, a geat art, but not everyone is a great animator. I was fascinated with it, but, coming from a ranch, I found it claustrophobic. Spending a lot of time in dark rooms, doing this very, very patient stuff, wasn't part of my nature, so the first live-action films I made were a holiday from this. I guess it was a desperate effort to get out into the sunshine again.

Gerald Potterton: Colin was talking about claustrophobia in animation and I agree with him one hundred percent. I was always split right down the middle between animation and live action. About 1954, there was this incredible London smog. People were dropping dead from the great killer-smogs. Well, I stumbled into one of those news theatres on Piccadilly, and saw these National Film Board films. There was a Crawley film called *Welcome to Yoho Valley*. I'd never been out of England. I think there actually is a Yoho Valley somewhere out near Vancouver. It's incredible, the Canada you imagine if you're a foreigner, sweeping, magnificent Rockies, the tumbling rivers, and all that — it's *Boys' Own Manual* Canada. In another incredible animated film called *The Romance of Transportation*, which Colin, Bob, and Tom made, there was this beautiful clean continent out there, and it was so fresh and simple and refreshing. Obviously the Film Board people were doing their job. They were pushing Canada to the world. Those two films made a very strong impression on me. I'd just gotten out of the RAF, and it seemed terrific to forget all this old London nonsense, borrow some money from the government, and get on a ship and come to Canada, which is what I did, actually. I thought, I want to get a job with the Film Board, wherever it is. When I found it was in Ottawa, I went there, and there were all these young guys running around in this amazing place on the edge of the Ottawa River. It was just fantastic.

Peter Harcourt: At the same time, Richard Williams was going to England.

Gerald Potterton: That's right. As a matter of fact, a year later I went back and met Richard. He came to the studios with these thousands of pieces of paper for this story board for *The Little Island*, a feature film he was going to make. It was a big feature animation-cinemascope film. We told him he was crazy, but he made it. A few years later it was finished. The animation department in Canada seemed like a terrific place. I've never regretted working with people like Bob, Colin, Tom, Wolf, and Roman. When you're young, in your twenties, and pretty naïve, it's a pretty powerful combination, especially if every five or six years you met somebody like John Grierson, who tells them all what a lot of bullshit it is, that they should forget everything they've learned and start all over again. Grierson did that. He was a great character to meet for bringing everything down to something brand-new again. I don't know if he really appreciated animation. He thought we were all crazy sitting in these dark rooms, drawing away, scratching, but I think that was to bring you down a bit. He would occasionally give you a shock like that.

Colin Low: I remember the day you came to the Film Board. Gerry had his portfolio of cartoons, and he had come all the way from England to work. There were about eight of us. I looked at the portfolio, and the cartoons were funny, very, very funny. The drawings were funny, and the ideas were funny. We had a film called *Fish Spoilage Control*, about how to treat your fish so they wouldn't rot. Who was the producer?

Gerald Potterton: Can I say something about *Fish Spoilage Control?* I was at a Cambridge animation festival. I don't go to festivals, but this year there was this animated feature, a film called *Heavy Metal*, in which about one thousand people worked. John Hallis was there from Hallis and Batchelor. He said, "Oh, Gerry, there's someone from Paris here who wants to meet you very much," and this French chap came running over. All he could talk about was *Fish Spoilage Control*, made in 1955. That's the truth!

Colin Low: But Gerry, you worked on that picture, and it was very fresh.

Gerald Potterton: It was the first film in which we had lip synchronization. We had one line at the end of the film. There was a man eating a piece of fish saying, "Fresh fish. Delish." We were so proud of that. Miracle.

Peter Harcourt: Am I not right in thinking that, when Grierson set up the Board, he was very concerned to have the animation section established from the outset? It wasn't just to do maps, though that was obviously important, and he was into maps. But I read something that said he wanted a division within the Board where film-makers could do films just for their own sake. For all his belief in propaganda, he believed that there should be this section where film could be used like clay, for its own sake. But I'm still interested in this influence on the documentary, and that's what I've been asked to address the panel towards. Does it take a different kind of mind to sit in a dark room and invent graphic images and play with graphic images? It certainly takes a different kind of mind to go out and talk to Paul Anka or Warren McCullough, or to some of these people who were interviewed in the course of making films for Unit B. I can't imagine Norman McLaren talking to Warren McCullough, somehow or other.

Margaret Ann Elton: Everyone forgets that Norman McLaren had some mastery in black-and-white live film, and he made an absolutely splendid film called *Book Market*, a compiling of the London telephone directory. Perhaps his only token documentary film, not animated.

Peter Harcourt: I'm trying to establish different scales, and different kinds of ways — introspective thinking, extroverted thinking — which go into one form of film as opposed to the other form of film, and whether or not part of the distinction of the National Film Board of Canada is that they have both been going on at the same time.

Colin Low: We've talked a lot in the last day or two about contradictons within Grierson. One of the most awesome and marvellous experiences was being connected with the contradictions of McLaren. On one side, there is a graphic sort of genius for intimate detail and, at the same time, an incredible sense of social interest. I don't know whether it's schizophrenic, but I think the roots of "Challenge for Change" and the international interest in the National Film Board can be traced through McLaren. When he left the Film Board in the late forties, he went to China to do one of those early projects using graphics in *The Healthy Village*, an early

United Nations project. Then he returned and talked to us about his experiences in China at the same time beginning to draft *Neighbours*. That was bound to be unsettling for the young people, unsettling but fascinating. There were a lot of things happening and there were a lot of people working in the animation department, people like Dino Rigelow, who went to Haiti, Herb Taylor, who went to South-East Asia, and Graham Crabtree, who was indirectly connected with the Film Board, but from Crawley's.

Gerald Potterton: Later we established the Ghana production unit, largely animation, and then Grierson became involved in the India project, also largely animation.

Colin Low: There's a continuity connecting the usefulness of animation and that which is peculiar to McLaren. He would do things that seemed so personal, and so nutty on one side, then swing one hundred eighty degrees to confront the world with —

Gerald Potterton: With *Neighbours* —

Colin Low: Yes, world issues, with quixotic abandon, and that was hard to relate to, but it had a very powerful influence on me.

Peter Harcourt: The film you've just seen, *City of Gold*, is technically made from still photographs, though ultimately it's an animation film. It's framed with live-action footage, you match the light, you match the feeling of the photographic image, and, I think, if it had not been those two elements going on, that film couldn't have been done as well as it was done. Indeed, the special effects for *Universe*, in one sense, were in the same way for all the people who saw it at Expo '67 created and recreated in the central chamber of *Labyrinth*. It gave a similar kind of effect of going into space. I don't mean to privilege one form of film-making over another, I just thought it was rare to find people working in both kinds of film with such success in each.

Colin Low: A lot of those developments had a kind of economic factor. McLaren was austere on one side; for instance, he used and re-used his cardboard. I've never seen anyone who was so Scottish and frugal in his use of materials. Sometimes McLaren's frugality was disheartening. There wasn't much money to do elaborate animation, what McLaren referred to as assembly-line animation, like the Hollywood mass-production thing. That was anathema to McLaren, because he was an old-fashioned, old-style, Scottish craftsman. From our work with maps and diagrams, we began to refine the animation camera and animation technology. Things like *City of Gold* came out of that certain kind of economy of means.

143

It seemed economical at the time. It wasn't necessarily an economic film but an economy of means. The first film of its type was *Age of the Beaver*. It used static materials to cover the history because there was no idea that we would be able to do dramatic history.

Peter Harcourt: Yes, McLaren was a master of the economical approach.

Forsyth Hardy: Let me pick up on this point about frugality. McLaren's very first films were actually made by scraping the emulsion off, and painting directly onto the celluloid. I was sitting beside Grierson when we first saw this film entered. One was made from painting directly onto the celluloid and, when Grierson saw this, he grasped my arm (I've still got the dent) and said, "Who made these?" I told him a little about the man. That was the beginning of the contact between Grierson and McLaren. The other film was about life at the Glasgow School of Art, called *Seven till Five*, or something of the kind. It was full of amateurish camera tricks, and shooting long and short. Grierson was aghast at this film because he thought it was full of sexual symbolism. Grierson took him off and gave him a proper wigging about making a film full of sexual symbolism, and that certainly put Norman off. Even so, as Lady Elton says, he went on to make *Book Market* in London. The link between Grierson and Norman is one of the most fascinating stories in the whole history of the film. Norman went first of all to the GPO in London where he was given this documentary kind of film to make. Laterly he had the opportunity also of making *Love on the Wing*, which was the beginning of the examination. Later, he went to Spain and worked with Ivor Montague. This was part of his political thing, which came out in a different form later when he went to China. That experience was reflected in *Neighbours* at a later stage. He was making commercial films in New York when Grierson brought him to Ottawa to become part of the Film Board. The full inter-relationship between the two men is utterly fascinating. I think it would have happened anyway, but it appeared stronger because both men came from Stirling. I'm delighted that the National Film Board of Canada has endowed a couple of seats in the new film house in Edinburgh, one in the name of Grierson, and the other in the name of Norman McLaren.

One more thing — I've brought this little book, which contains little details about McLaren. It's not an in-depth study, more of a future book, with a lot of archival photos, which have been lent by the Board and other institutions. Interested people could ask their Film Board offices about it.

Margaret Ann Elton: May I add to Forsyth Hardy's remarks that, after Norman's return from the UNESCO China visit, where he worked on the film project *Healthy Village*, I met him in Paris. In the normal civil-service way, he was required to present a report to UNESCO. All government agencies, national, international, provincial, and local, ask for a report. Norman's report seemed to have no letters, or no writing. Instead, he wrote his report in terms of 35mm frames on which he had drawn the account. I'd like to know what UNESCO made of it, and in what dusty file this great report of stewardship now lies.

Tom Daly: Sometimes, when we were explaining our high-jinks to some of the sober heads of information in government departments, we took an approach that gained a laugh rather than a groan. It helped do the job better. The court jester, of course, was Grierson.

Gerald Potterton: In the twenties, in the time of the old Max Sennett films, they used to have those old gag conferences. There'd be all these fairly straight-laced writers and people, so they'd throw in a wild man. That's what they called him. Suddenly he would say something that had absolutely nothing to do with the discussion. Occasionally it worked. Now, in Norman's case, it nearly always worked. I'm sure it was something similar.

Colin Low: Internationally, in animation there has been public acceptance. It's very similar to the political cartoon, and it's highly cost-effective. When you say a film is going to cost X dollars, it sounds a lot, but in terms of its life-span and audience reach, it is very cost-effective. So part of the survival capacity of animation in the Film Board rests on the original frugality.

Gerald Potterton: It tends to date less quickly than the live-action film, also. I don't know why. In live action, cars, costumes, and so on change quickly, but an animated character has a fairly good life, if it's funny.

David Balcon: Animation — as opposed to what we saw in *City of Gold* — tends to rely on using metaphors and symbols to get the messages across. Yesterday Colin said that, to make an effective film, he liked to use straight documentary interview. Do you think there is a way for metaphorical language to be used in an animation film as a universal statement?

Colin Low: Oh, sure, David, I think it's possible, but it is outside my own skill and talent. I know that now. I didn't realize it earlier. Recently the Film Board made a child film called *Every Child*. It's a metaphor and obviously has a very broad audience. I can see the same thing being done in relationship to race. The film you saw yesterday was intensely local. It had some ramifications outside the situation, but was mostly local.

David Balcon: For those purposes, the Film Board needs different forms of expression to get across messages of propaganda.

Colin Low: Well, a film like *Propaganda Message* is effective because people understand the nuances. It's done in French and English. French and English find it equally funny. It's sub-titled and, therefore, immediately accessible to a very broad audience. It certainly has much to do with race, or culture, or bi-culture, but the producers understand the difficulties. Being involved as producer of both kinds of films, I see that there are two special things about animation. One is that actuality can deal only with what has already been put into actual practice in the world. It cannot deal with visions that have not yet come into being. With animation, you can go into that whole world. It may be just as real as what is now actual, but you are not restricted. You can deal with inferior, difficult, and touchy things, through animation, engagingly and deeply.

Peter Harcourt: I think we've been running late all day, so let's just wrap this up. We have another exciting session involving music — music for film — coming up. We'll take a short break now and then start the next session. Thank you very much.

ELDON RATHBURN

The NFB: Sounds and Music

ELDON RATHBURN, who wrote more than three hundred musical scores for the NFB, chose a selection of scores to play for the audience. For each film score, he gave a short introduction.

Capital Plan (1949)
The Gréber Plan — it was a plan to beautify the city of Ottawa with relocation of factories, and better recreational facilities, and so on. The music relates to the main title. It was played by an orchestra of about twenty-two men, which was considered to be a large orchestra in those days. The film was one of the "Canada Carries On" series and, since it was theatrical, it was necessary to be as impressive as possible. This was a difficult feat because the end music of a Hollywood feature preceding the CCO probably had a score using up to seventy-five players.

As the pub has its old piano, the circus its calliope, Parliament Hill has its carillon. We recorded it on disc, later transferring it to optical film. All kinds of difficulties occurred during the recording of the carillon, including traffic noise, wind, and frayed tempers. The climax of it all was my being fined by the union for using a non-union man to play the carillon. How was I to know that there was a line-up of unemployed carillon players walking the streets of Ottawa?

Here Is Canada (1972)
Made twenty-three years later, this film is a gentler, non-aggressive look at our country. The mosaic approach was employed, not the sea-to-sea method, or what I used to call the "Octave Leap," Newfoundland, of course, being middle C. This music is the end-title music. A lighter sound than the *Capital Plan* music is evident; it is more transparent. The commentary style

had become more casual, too, not the driving style used in earlier films.

The Hecklers (1975)
A history of political cartoons, this film is designed to put much emphasis on Canadian ones. Again we used the carillon, but this time as a solo instrument, and I received no fine from the union. I want to add here that the use of fewer instruments in a film was often due to financial restraints. In a way this was a blessing. As a composer, one learned that mere quantity of sound doesn't ever make up for lack of quality in an effective score.

Thunder in the East (1950)
This is a film about the Korean War. We used all kinds of ominous music, relieved, at times, with "positive" music relating to the good guys at the UN. The familiar brassy fanfare, which is used to indicate that trouble is brewing, can be heard. Incidentally, I myself have always found it easier to write ominous music rather than happy music. When writing a happy or "positive" score, it is easy to get into all kinds of musical trouble. Happy music can easily become too cute, and positive music can get sentimental. When I was at the NFB I always wanted to write some romantic love music, but the subjects of my films were never suitable, and I was prevented from it. I had to write about soil erosion, insects, labour relations, fish, or mental illness, subjects not in keeping with romantic music.

Enemy Alien (1975)
The music in this film is about the main title. It depicts a look backward at the internment of the Japanese in Canada during the last war. Following immediately after the title, flashbacks of war scenes are seen on the screen. I tried to obtain a dramatic effect, one that was more inward than the music of *Thunder in the East*. Since the film is about the past, I used a smaller orchestra because a big sound was not needed.

Heroes (1976)
This film concerns the psychological damage suffered by soldiers returning from the war. This is the title music. I tried to combine two ideas — camaraderie and dissolution. It took me back to the

early days when I was sometimes asked to write some "sad" music with "happy" overtones. In this film, there is "happy" music with "sad" undertones. One of the things I find fascinating in writing music is trying to combine different moods in music. In the film *City of Gold*, I combined ragtime with a sombre bass ostinato. Today we cannot escape listening to combinations of different sounds. It is part of our life.

Teeth Are To Keep (1949)
This film was made for children. The characters are all in the style of "Peanuts." The music was used for a young boy and his dog who are engaged in a friendly chase. Everything about it is cute and light-hearted. A four-piece musical group was used.

The Romance of Transportation (1952)
In this year of 1952, "bop" was in the air. I decided to use a group of jazz men for the score. Although the film covers the early days of transportation, I used contemporary music. I remember how hard I had to fight off the temptation to use tom-toms over an Indian-canoe sequence. The combination of humorous animation, a dry, almost "prissy" commentary, and jazz music made this an interesting film. In a way, it could be called a three-part invention.

Fields of Space (1969)
All animation films need not be humorous. Animation is certainly the best answer for films about space. The orchestra here is small. It consists of piano, celeste, harp, Hammond organ, alto flute, percussion, and a wordless voice. You won't hear it here.

Canon (1964)
The musical form of the canon gets a real workout in this film, both pictorially and musically. All the variations are used here, augmentation, diminution, retrograde, inversions, and so on. I am sure that, if there was a way to do a hexagonal version, Norman McLaren would have found it. The elements used in the score were the piano, clavichord, guitar, percussion, synthetic sound, as well as a few sound effects. The synthetic sound is Norman McLaren's own invention. The sound waves were painted on cards, which were photographed under the animation camera. Each note had its own card. The attacks and decays, as well as the rests, had to be

carefully worked out. Needless to say, the shooting of synthetic sound demands a lot of concentration. I remember much talking to myself in order to keep my mind fixed on the work at hand. The music you are now hearing occurs near the end of the film.

ANDERSON, ROBERT: announcer, CBC; head, TV Production, NFB; freelance film director and producer, Robert Anderson Associates, Ltd., Ottawa. NFB films include the *Mental Mechanism* series, *The Feeling of Hostility, The Feeling of Rejection, Overdependency, Les Bannis imaginaires.*

ANSTEY, DAPHNE: involved in early NFB, negative cutting, the production of *Country Women of the World.*

ANSTEY, EDGAR: British documentary filmmaker, director, producer, university lecturer, film critic; member, Empire Marketing Board Film Unit, 1931; creator, Shell Film Unit, 1934; producer, Film Centre, 1938; head, British Transport Film Unit, 1949-1974. NFB films include *Enough to Eat?, Coal Crisis, March of Time* series, *This Modern Age*; and numerous industrial and transport films in Britain, the U.S. and for the U.N.

APPLEBAUM, LOUIS, O.C., LL.D.: international concert and film composer, conductor, writer, university lecturer; joined NFB in 1941; Canadian arts administrator, including chairman, Canadian Federal Culture Policy Review Committee. Over 200 film scores include *Tomorrow the World, The Story of G.I. Joe, March of Time* series. Numerous awards for film music and contributions to the Canadian arts.

BEATTIE, ELEANOR: Author of two editions of *The Handbook of Canadian Film*, university lecturer in film in Canada and Slade School, London. Thesis on Harold Pinter's drama and film scripts.

BEVERIDGE, JAMES: founding member of NFB; documentary filmmaker in Canada, the U.S., India and Japan. Developed rural television in Poona, India, under UNESCO; university lecturer at New York University and York University, Toronto. NFB films include *A is for Architecture, Battle of the Harvest, Break Through, Great Lakes, Highways North, Look to the North, North Sea, Pulp and Paper from Canada, Eye Witness Industrial, Land for Pioneers.*

CAYA, MARCEL, Ph.D.: Archivist, PAC, Ottawa; University Archivist, McGill University. Thesis on Canadian history.

CHIASSON, RODRIGUE: Director-General, Research Branch, Canadian Radio-television and Telecommunications Commission, and presently with the Government of New Brunswick.

CHISHOLM, ELSPETH: radio broadcaster, documentary journalist, teacher; production and research officer, English Section, NFB, 1963-66. Hon. consultant to the John Grierson Project, McGill University, 1978- ; Adviser, John Grierson Conference, McGill University, 1981. Film productions include *Experience Hands*, NFB; frequent contributions to CBC's *Take Thirty*. Radio documentaries include: *The Indian Summer of John Grierson, H.A. Innis; Alan Jarvis; Henri Bourassa, André Laurendeau.*

COX, KIRWIN: freelance producer, consultant, including chairman, Council of Canadian Filmmakers, university lecturer; director, Research and Policy Development, NFB, 1980- . Films produced include histories of Canadian cinema: *Dreamland, Has Anyone Here Seen Canada?*

CRAWLEY, JUDITH and BUDGE: writers, film animators, directors, producers, NFB and Crawley Films, Ottawa, from the 1930s. Numerous films produced include *The Loon's Necklace, The Man Who Skiied Down Everest* (Academy Award, 1975); films for television and Expo 67; awards from Canada, Edinburgh, Venice, Chicago, and so on.

DALY, TOM: documentary filmmaker, editor, script writer, director, executive producer, NFB, 1940-84. Activities include founding the Stock Shot Library, NFB, 1941, editor-in-chief, *Labyrinth*, Expo 67. More than 500 films produced include *Hungry Minds, Ordeal By Ice, Feeling of Depression, Longhouse People, Canada's Awakening North, Family Tree, V for Volunteer, Corral, City of Gold, Circle of the Sun, Glenn Gould On/Off the Record, Universe, Lonely Boy, Labyrinth, Action/Reaction: The October Crisis of 1970, Mr. Symbol Man, North China Commune. From the Ashes of War, The Last Days of the Living, F.R. Scott, Earle Birney, Off the Wall, Standing Alone, The Wars.* Awards: too numerous to mention.

ELLIS, JACK, Ed.D.: writer, consultant, university lecturer in film studies; founding chairman, Department of Radio, Television and Film School of Speech, Northwestern University. Writings included in *Film Study in Higher Education, Canadian Film Reader*; editor, *The Film Book Bibliography, A History of Film, John Grierson: A Guide to References and Resources, Cinema Journal*, 1976- .

ELTON, MARGARET ANN (Lady Elton): documentary film-maker, early NFB, lecturer, writer, keeper of the Elton Archives, England. Films include *Iceland on the Prairies, Country Women of the World.*

GULKIN, HARRY: journalist, consultant, independent film producer, Gulkin Associates; films and awards include *Lies My Father Told Me, Jacob Two-Two Meets the Hooded Fang, Two Solitudes.*

HARCOURT, PETER: writer, broadcaster, film director and producer. Assistant education officer, BFI, London, 1962-67; university lecturer and chairman, Department of Film, Queen's University, 1967-74; York University, 1974- . Films include: *Vaghy, Production: Dance, Antonioni*; writings include *Six European Directors, Movies and Mythologies: towards a national cinema.*

HARDY, FORSYTH, O.B.E.: writer, journalist, critic, film producer; chairman, Arts Review for BBC Scotland; co-founder and Hon. Vice-President, Edinburgh International Film Festival, the Edinburgh Film House; Hon. Advisor to the Grierson Archive, Stirling University, Scotland. Writings include *John Grierson, A Documentary Biography, John Grierson's Scotland, Filmgoers' Review, Scandinavian Film*; editor, *Grierson on Documentary, Grierson on the Movies.* Film productions include over 150 films for Scottish government departments and the Films of Scotland Committee, including the Oscar winner *Seawards the Great Ships.*

LOCKERBIE, IAN Ph.D.: Professor and Chairman, Department of French, Stirling University, Scotland; Chairman, the John Grierson Archive, Stirling University. Teaching and research in French language, literature, film studies; Past Chairman Scottish Film Council; Chairman, Scottish Film Production Fund. Publications include writings on Charles Cros, Guillarme Apollinaire, John Grierson.

LOW, COLIN, LL.D.: graphic artist, documentary filmmaker, director and executive producer, NFB, 1945- , including head, Animation Department, 1950-65, designer and co-director, Labyrinth, Expo 67; initiator of Challenge for Change series and 3D-computerized movie technology. Numerous films and awards include *Age of the Beaver, Romance of Transportation, Corral, City of Gold, Circle of the Sun, The Hutterites, Universe,* the *Challenge for Change* series, the *Fogo Island* series, *Nell and Fred, The Sea, New Alchemist, Cree Hunters of Mistassini, Biosphere, Standing Alone*; films for IMAX and OMNIMAX. Awards too numerous to list include the Grierson Award.

OHLIN, PETER, Ph.D.: writer, university lecturer, Department of English, McGill University, 1964- ; director, NFB-McGill Summer Research Institute in Film Studies, 1967-72 and the Grierson Conference, McGill University, 1981. Writings include *Agee, The Self-Reflexive Film: Its Narrative Crisis 1960-1970.*

PARSONS, BRENDA: Assistant to the Director, Graduate Program in Communications, McGill University; editor and research co-ordinator, John Grierson Project, McGill University, 1978- . Thesis on John Grierson's *Drifters.*

POTTERTON, GERALD: film animator, writer, director, NFB, 1954-1967; president, writer, director of feature and children's films for television, Potterton Productions, Montreal, 1968- ; films and awards include *My Financial Career, Christmas Cracker, The Railrodder* (Belgian, London, 1965), *Pinter People* (Chicago, 1969), *The Rainbow Boys* (Atlanta, 1973), *The Happy Prince, The Selfish Giant, Raggedy Ann and Andy,* and numerous others.

RATHBURN, ELDON, L.M.: musician, lecturer, film composer, freelance and NFB, 1947-1976. Scores include *Labyrinth,* Expo 67, *City of Gold, Aspects of Railroads, The Metamorphic Ten.*

ROBSON, NORA: writer, co-ordinator/editor, Grierson Conference McGill University, 1981. Thesis in Canadian literature.

SPARLING, GORDON: filmmaker, director, producer, 1924- ; director, Canadian Cameo Company; producer, NFB 1957-66.

Some 200 films include *Carry on Sergeant!, Ballet of the Mermaids, The Breadwinner, Grey Owl's Little Brother, The Mapleville Story, Music from the Stars, Those Other Days, Sitzmarks the Spot, Peoples of Canada.*

SPENCER, MICHAEL: Film director and editor; NFB, 1940-41; Canadian Army Film Unit, 1941-46; producer, NFB, 1946-53; head of the Liaison Division, NFB Ottawa, 1953-60; director of planning, NFB Montreal 1960-66; creator and first Director, Canadian Film Development Corporation, 1968-78; freelance producer and consultant, 1978- .

VERRAL, ROBERT: animation filmmaker, founding member, NFB animation department, 1941 and later director, English production. Films and awards include *The Romance of Transportation, Structure of Unions, A is for Architecture, The Great Toy Robbery, Energy and Matter, What on Earth* (4 international awards), *The Drag, Pikangikum, Tax is not a Four Letter Word, Broomsville, Population Explosion, Energy and Matter, Cosmic Zoom.*

WRIGHT, BASIL: British documentary film director, producer, lecturer; founding member, Empire Marketing Board Film Unit, 1929, Realist Film Unit, 1937, Film Centre, 1938; active in both Britain and Canada from 1939 on. Film producer, Film Centre and Crown Film Unit during WW II; producer, International Realist, 1946 onwards. Films include *Windmill in Barbados, Song of Ceylon, Night Mail*; London editor of *World in Action, Canada Carries On* series; *Waters of Time, World Without End, The Immortal Land, A Place for Gold.* Author of a history of film, *The Long View: A Personal Perspective on World Cinema.*